The Bible says "Love is not arrogant or rude."
How rude can a wife be when she doesn't let her husband
be the gentleman he wants to be!
And on the other hand, how rude can a husband be when he
doesn't show enough love for his wife to be concerned!
The Bible says "Love rejoices in the right."
It's right to have a happy marriage. And it's right
to be fun to live with.
Think of yourself right now. Are you honestly fun
to live with?

How to make your MARRIAGE EXCITING

By Charles Frances Hunter

G/L REGAL BOOKS

A Division of G/L Publications
Glendale, California U.S.A.

Other books by Frances Hunter—

My Love Affair with Charles
Hot Line to Heaven
God Is Fabulous
Go, Man, Go!
P.T.L.A. (Praise the Lord Anyway)
Hang Loose with Jesus
The Two Sides of a Coin
Since Jesus Passed By

A cassette seminar is available by Frances ♥♥ Charles
Hunter on how to make your marriage exciting.

Scripture quotations are taken from:
The Authorized Version (KJV)
New American Standard Bible. ©The Lockman Foundation, 1971.
Used by permission.
The Living Bible, Paraphrased (Wheaton: Tyndale House,
Publishers, 1971). Used by permission.

Second printing, 1972
Third printing, 1972
Fourth printing, 1973
Fifth printing, 1973
Sixth printing, 1974
Seventh printing, 1975

Published by
Regal Books Division, G/L Publications
Glendale, California 91209, U.S.A.
Library of Congress Catalog Card No. 79-180988
ISBN 0-8307-0147-8

Dedicated to God, who created

marriage and to whom we give thanks

for this beautiful relationship

Contents

Prologue

A cassette seminar is available by Frances ♡♡ Charles Hunter on how to make your marriage exciting.

Prologue

"Then the Lord God formed man of dust from the ground, and breathed into his nostrils the breath of life; and man became a living being. . . . Then the Lord God said, 'It is not good for the man to be alone; I will make him a helpmeet suitable for him'" (Genesis 2:7,18).

"So the Lord God caused a deep sleep to fall upon the man, and he slept; then He took one of his ribs, and closed up the flesh at that place. And the Lord God fashioned into a woman the rib which He had taken from the man, and brought her to the man. And the man said, 'This is now bone of my bones, and flesh of my flesh; She shall be called Woman, because she was taken out of Man.' For this cause a man shall leave his father and his mother, and shall cleave to his wife; and they shall become one flesh" (Genesis 2:21-24).

God had created the universe and with His wonderful sovereign power, He created all the things in it. Picture in your mind your own beginning, because actually your very beginning started when God created the heavens and the earth. If you can possibly comprehend, even to a small degree, the power that was represented in the creation, remember that it is the same mighty power which raised Christ from the dead, and the same mighty power of God that created you.

After God had created all the heavens and the earth, the day and night, the waters, the light and the dark, the vegetation, the creatures of the sea, the birds of the air, the animals of the earth, then He said, "Let us make man in our image, according to our likeness; and let them rule over . . . all the earth . . ." (Genesis 1:26). And so with hands of love and a desire that His last creation would be the most superior of all, in all ways, God skillfully and lovingly took the simple dust of the earth and from this began molding what was to be man, the thing He was creating in His own image.

Think how carefully God planned and molded every single little detail of man. Think how He lovingly and beautifully constructed a brain; a brain that would be capable of being superior to every other thing placed on the earth, having dominion over all. Think of the beauty of the moment when God finished molding the perfect body for man. Think how God must have looked at and loved this creature, this man, whom He had made in His very own image. Think how God must have caressed him as He drew him close, and then in that great moment of tenderness and love, breathed into his nostrils the very breath of life.

Can you imagine God right now so close to you that His very breath can be felt by you as He breathes life into you? Can you imagine the love of God at that great moment, when His breath was put into the first human body to give it life? God breathed His very life into man!

I remember those precious moments when my children were born, when I heard their first cries, and I knew that life was in them. How my cup bubbled over with joy! I felt at that moment, in a very small way, how God must have felt as He drew close to Him the body He had created and breathed the breath of life into it, because then and only then did man become a living soul.

Then God said, "It is not good for the man to be alone; I will make him a helpmeet suitable for him." God planned that in marriage the woman would be a helper, not a hindrance, for man.

I think it's extremely interesting how God made woman. He could have taken a little pinch of dirt and just said "poof" and created woman, but He didn't do it that way. Instead, He caused a deep sleep to fall upon Adam, and while he was sleeping, God skillfully made an incision and removed one of his ribs, and from this He created woman. God chose to make the woman from an actual physical part of the man so that forever they should be one flesh. God intended from the very beginning that man's helpmeet should be an actual part of him— not a separate being, but exactly the same flesh and bone that he was.

Adam and Eve were given an absolutely perfect marriage and it remained perfect until they sinned against God. It is possible for every married couple to enjoy this same perfect relationship today. God gave us in this physical story of the Garden of Eden a spiritual story of truth. You see, Jesus is the garden where all is perfect when He fully controls our life, our actions and our thoughts—our marriage. Jesus is the tree of life which grew physically in the garden and He is the Tree of Life as He provides the fruit we eat and become; the only fruit needed for a perfect life—for a perfect marriage is: love, joy, peace, patience, kindness, faithfulness, goodness; against such things there is no law—there is perfection—there is JESUS! Would you like to move back into the Garden of Eden in your marriage? Then come with us.

This book is written with a desire for marriage to return to the original plan for which God created it. We have asked you to visualize a loving God actually breathing new life into you, as He breathed life into Adam. But we hope you won't fall into the same old trap that Adam and Eve fell into after this happens.

Eve was tempted and she ate the fruit from the tree of knowledge of good and evil and then shared it with her husband. The Bible doesn't specifically say how she talked him into eating it, or maybe it was just a gesture of love to want to share everything with him, but watch what happened when they discovered they had been caught. Immediately Adam blamed Eve, and Eve blamed the serpent. And it's been the same through the centuries. But it doesn't need to be so. In the same way that God breathed His life into Adam and he became a living soul, so Christ will breathe Himself into your marriage, and your marriage can become a *living* marriage the way God intended for it to be.

As you open this book, read how we could have

fallen into the same trap as Adam and Eve did, and then read how God has touched our marriage. As you read some of the trapdoors which could have caught us, see how they apply to your own marriage. When you have finished reading may your eyes have been opened as to how you can really make your marriage exciting.

Be Honest

by Frances

Would it surprise you if I told you there is a great percentage of adults today who are married—AND LIKE IT? I know it wouldn't surprise you at all if I told you there are many unhappy marriages in America today. I just feel an urge to remind people how exciting marriage can really be, and to see if those of us who like the institution of marriage can pass on to others how any marriage can be transformed into an exciting way of life.

This book is designed to show the things to do, and not the "no-no's" of marriage. I am always on the positive side of everything, so it seemed the thing to do was to name the chapters the *BE* Attitudes. Charles and I have discovered these are the secrets to a marriage that's happy, exciting, loving, stimulating, satisfying, romantic and every other adjective you can think of to describe marriage in the way God intended it to be.

All of the *BE* Attitudes are important to a happy marriage. As I looked over the chapter titles, I tried to pick which one was the most important, and it was a hard decision because I don't know if any one is really more important than all the others, or if they all work in conjunction with each other. Then I thought about my car. The engine is real important, but it wouldn't do me any good if I didn't have wheels on the car, would it? And so the wheels are important. But the wheels wouldn't do me much good if I didn't have a steering apparatus, would they? And so on down the line. But there must be a start somewhere, and it seems to me this little matter of being honest can do as much for marriage as anything else. This simple little "Be" attitude can stop many problems before they become serious.

When Charles came to Miami for our marriage, we had no time to discover a lot of things about each other, as many couples do, because of our unusual courtship (told in the book, *My Love Affair with Charles*). But one of the first things Charles said to me was, "I want us to be completely honest with each other at all times. I don't want us even to hold back a piece of a thought from each other."

I'll have to be honest with you, that statement really shocked me. I wish I could recall all the thoughts that went through my mind concerning this request. My first thought was that I could never tell him anything that might hurt his feelings. Suppose he asked me if I liked his tie, wouldn't it be permissible to say "yes" even if I thought it was terrible, just to make him happy? And while he was insistent that honesty was a must in our marriage, and I reluctantly agreed, I have to admit I was secretly thinking, "That might be all right for you, but I don't know if it's all right with me."

Have any of you women ever bought a dress that you paid too much for, and then decided you were going to save the money out of the grocery money, and not tell *him* how much it cost? Have you ever sneaked a little money out to buy something you or the kids wanted, but you were afraid to tell *him* the truth about it? Well, then maybe you can understand my feelings at that moment. I felt there might be little situations come up where it would be easier if I just forgot to mention them to Charles, and so I started off not being honest with him right then because I didn't tell him that I didn't really think that would work.

Sin is such a sneaky little character. Sometimes we do not even recognize it in the beginning for what it really is. And because all of us, even those who spend twenty-four hours a day talking about God and Christ Jesus are subject to the devil-darts, I want to relate to you how a "little bitty" sin almost turned out to be a monster; I want you to notice where it hit—in the area in my life you'd least suspect it to hit.

I received a call from the San Antonio Christian Woman's Club to speak at their meeting on one of my open dates. I accepted and told Charles, and this was fine with him. Everything was great. A couple of nights later I mentioned to him that I thought I would stay overnight in San Antonio in the event one of the churches there wanted me to speak when they heard I was going to be in town. Charles didn't exactly like the idea of my being away from home because we had been apart so much during our first year of marriage. He suggested that I fly to San Antonio, speak to the club there, and then fly back that afternoon. I wouldn't have to be away from home, and this could all be done while he was at the office working, so I agreed.

Then an interesting development occurred. The Christian Woman's Club in Austin called, having heard that I was going to be in San Antonio, and asked me to come one day earlier so I could speak to their club since I was so close to their town. I felt strongly that God had called me there, too. So I accepted because I knew it would mean I'd be away from home only for one night. I knew that Charles wouldn't mind because he backs me up all the time in my speaking engagements. But instead of calling Charles on the telephone and telling him immediately, I decided to wait until he got home that night and then explain to him that my acceptance of this date would mean that I would be gone for the one night. What really happened was I had done something I had told Charles I wouldn't do, and so, instinctively, I decided to wait and tell him at the right time. In my mind I rationalized that I would have his favorite dinner prepared and would serve it by candlelight when he came home that night. I would smother him with an unusual number of kisses so he would know that I loved him, and then I would tell him and everything would be fine.

Watch what happened! Charles had worked especially hard that day and was exceptionally tired. He had gotten up in the morning around five o'clock to start an early day. His work load had been extremely heavy, and he was exhausted when he came home. I smothered him with the usual number of kisses but because he was so tired I decided this wasn't the right time to tell him, so I said

5

nothing. I justified the action by saying to myself that I would tell him when the time was right. (The old devil is so clever in his nasty, sneaky way, because he really convinced me it would be bad to tell Charles when he was so tired, so I put it off for another night.) All through the next day I knew how I was going to tell Charles, the exact words I was going to use, the exact timing, and I anticipated putting on a little extra of my "Charles" perfume. So I knew everything was going to be all right, and it would have been had I told him.

But guess what happened! We had unexpected company the next night, so again I decided it wasn't the right time—because I had to fill him in on the details of the couple who was due for counseling at any minute (by the way, their main problem was a lack of honesty with each other). When they finally left our home, it was too late to tell Charles.

I really love Charles, and I didn't want to tell him anything that would hurt him, but by not telling him the very instant I accepted the booking, I was day by day creating a situation which could have been very unhealthy, even though such was not my intention at all. Then instead of telling Charles instantly, I began to bury that little dishonesty with my beloved husband and figured I would think of some way to tell him before long. But instead I buried it deeper and deeper because I didn't like how it made me feel when I thought about it. I felt real dirty inside, and just tucked the thought further and further back in my mind.

We continued talking in various churches and in

many marriage counseling sessions, and one of the things we stressed over and over was complete honesty. By this time the devil had so smoothed San Antonio over, I really didn't think about it too much until we got up to talk about the secrets of a happy marriage. When we reached the part about complete honesty with each other, I'd nearly die. Right on the spot I would send up a quick prayer to God saying, "Forgive me, God, for not being honest with Charles. I'll tell him on the way home tonight."

To get to our house from almost any place in Houston, we use a freeway. Now Houston is often called the "spaghetti" city because of our many wonderful freeways, all of which have very interesting names like West Loop, North Loop, South Loop, Gulf Freeway, etc., but would you like to know the name of the freeway we use to get home? There's only one, and it's called the San Antonio freeway. I would be reminded about not having told Charles every time one of the big freeway signs would appear that said, "San Antonio," only by this time it looked to me like "SIN" Antonio. I would just shudder inside and then I'd say, "Lord, now when we get home tonight, I'm going to tell Charles about San Antonio." But somehow or other when we got home the devil would assure me this wasn't the night to tell him, that a better night would be tomorrow, and so I wouldn't tell Charles.

Soon a month had elapsed, and I still hadn't told Charles. Occasionally Charles would refer to my speaking at the club and say, "I'm so glad you're not going to be gone overnight." Then I'd really cringe inside, but somehow or other the devil made me think that if I told Charles right then he might be mad at me, so I would tell God I'd tell him when "the time was right." It's a funny thing, though, now that I think about it—the devil *never* has a right time, does he?

We went on a trip to the Pacific Northwest, and things really began to happen. We continued speaking of complete honesty and every time we did, I was torn up inside, and then I'd say, "God, how am I going to tell him? How can I explain to him why I've held off so long telling him?" The horrible part of it all is that sin doesn't get better with age—it gets worse!

It seemed in every church where we spoke, in every college where we spoke, in every club where we spoke, in every denomination where we spoke, somewhere along the line the following conversation ensued, "So you're from Texas? What part? Houston, that's great. My hometown isn't very far from where you are." And of course, I would say "Where do you hail from?" And then I would cringe, because before they ever opened their mouths I would know their hometown! It just had to be SAN ANTONIO . . . and it was! And each time I would hear the name San Antonio, I nearly died. When I heard a car radio playing, it was "San Antonio Rose" or "Deep in the Heart of Texas" and I hadn't heard those songs for years. It seemed every airport we went into had a special on plane fare and the destination of all these specials was . . . you guessed it—San Antonio. What torture we put ourselves through when we are not completely honest.

Every time I would hear even the word "Texas" I was laden with guilt because I knew what would follow next, and the prospect of telling Charles became a bigger and bigger mountain all the time. And every time someone took us from one town to another we saw cars from Texas. I was convinced by this time that there was only one city in Texas, and that was San Antonio, because that's where all the cars seemed to be from.

We had a really unusual experience while we were on this trip. A young boy had felt God speak to him concerning the healing of his eyes, and both Charles and I had a great burden for this young man who had such tremendous faith. One night about 1:00 A.M. God's Holy Spirit woke me up and laid this young man right on my heart. I started praying, and before long, Charles woke up and he, too, joined me in prayer. We began talking about this young man, and God clearly indicated we should go to His Word, and so we did. After much reading and further praying for his healing, I prayed, "God, if there is any sin in my Doug's life, known or unknown, which stands in the way of his healing, reveal it to him, so that he can be forgiven and cleansed." Then I continued, "God, if there is any sin. . . ." And the words, "San Antonio," came out instantly. I had buried "San Antonio" deeply in my mind and wasn't even thinking about that when God's Holy Spirit brought it back into my mind. I threw my arms around Charles's neck, and in prayer to God, the whole story came pouring out and I asked God to see that Charles forgave me and to let him understand how things like this happen.

Naturally, there were tears as Charles laughed and loved me and said, "Honey, that's all right, you KNOW when God calls you it's always perfect with me!"

Now the horrible truth was out. After having kept it bottled up for such a long time, it came out in a moment of honest soul searching. As always, God's love prevailed, and it was no problem at all. But think of all the things that happened. Because I had not been totally honest with Charles from the word go, I had compounded the sin, had gone through misery beyond belief and was plagued by guilt. If I had simply told Charles in the first place that God was leading in my acceptance of this date, there would have been no question at all. And the funniest part is this, when I finally had the courage to look at that particular page in my date book, I discovered not only had I compounded that sin, I had re-compounded it, because I had accepted a third date and put it in my book without realizing it, which meant two nights away from home. That's the trouble with sin—one leads to another, and one bit of dishonesty creates another bit of dishonesty until it becomes impossible even to know when you're sinning. Well, we've got the slate clean now. God forgave me, Charles forgave me, and I learned a lesson.

Charles said it was not hard to forgive that time, but he said if I ever held something back or was dishonest again it would break his heart because then he might never be able to trust me enough to be sure I wasn't deceiving him.

Am I going to hold back even a little thought

from Charles ever again? You'd better believe I'm not! And to keep me remembering the lesson I learned, is the sign I have to pass every time I drive in or out of our home which says "San Antonio." Today I look at the sign and laugh, but I don't see the words it has printed on it, I only see the words, "Be honest!"

by Charles

Frances asked me how I came upon the idea that being completely honest with each other throughout our marriage was so vital that I challenged both of us to be totally honest with each other, even to a thought or a piece of a thought.

This desire for real honesty apparently started in my deep search for God's plan for my life. I began to question myself as to how I could be completely honest with God. I found myself saying, "God, I'm sorry for the thought I just had." Then I would say, "God, am I just saying words or do I really mean I'm sorry enough to want you not only to forgive me, but to take any desire out of my mind about a recurrence of the thought?"

I began to see that I often said just words and didn't really have a genuine repentance about my asking forgiveness; that I didn't even have a sincere deep desire to have the sin removed—just a desire to admit it to God. Then I realized there was a great difference between just admitting something and of confessing with an attitude and desire to have all evidence of the sin removed. After about three months of talking to God and having Him give me plenty of opportunities to recognize that I really wasn't being honest with Him, I accepted a marvelous new way of life. And each time I really was sorry for being dishonest with Him, He would remove that sin from my life and once again I was free.

So, I was perfectly conditioned to being honest when Frances and I were married. Since I apply my relationship to God to every phase of my life, it was a very natural thing for me to want our relationship with each other to be the same as with God. Therefore I said to Frances, "Let's be totally honest with each other, even to telling each other every thought, even if it seems that it might hurt the other's feelings."

Being a business man who is often involved in the settlement of disagreements between members of a firm, I have discovered that once all the facts are out in the open where everyone involved on both sides can take a clear look at them, they are much easier to solve. I also have noticed that in business and in church business meetings people involved often make comments which are not quite complete. Generally this is so because they know an important factor in the problem and if they revealed the truth, someone might be hurt or might have their toes stepped on. Therefore the information presented is distorted or incomplete. Here are people trying to solve a problem honestly with dishonest facts. The result is always the same—a dishonest answer or multiplied problems. Think about what Frances just said about her "San Antonio" problem—each time she held back the truth, it multiplied her problems and never gave an answer.

Think about the attitude most of us have concerning the police. We instinctively think, "Maybe he didn't see me . . . maybe he didn't notice I was going over the speed limit." Shouldn't we instead be glad to see a policeman? If we are truly honest, we will know that he is there for our own good. It's when we are trying to cover up a little driving sin that we don't want him to see us because we don't want to face the truth. ". . . The policeman does not frighten people who are doing right; but those doing evil will always fear him. So if you don't want to be afraid, keep the laws and you will get along well. The policeman is sent by God to help you" (Romans 13:3).

God's Holy Spirit was sent by Christ Jesus to help us, and if we are honest with Him, there will be no desire in our hearts for dishonesty with anyone. If something inadvertently comes into our lives which causes us to be tempted not to tell our beloved spouse, then we can be pretty sure it *should* be told to them, because anything that seems wrong, *is* wrong. Frances's and my relationship has been strengthened every time we share with each other something we find hard to make ourselves tell.

Since knowing you are always going to tell your spouse the truth about a situation, you naturally will think seriously before you get involved in a wrong. The more I am involved with Frances in abiding by our promise (not a legalistic promise, but a promise made because we wanted to make it and keep it) the more I am aware of the importance and application of it in our relationship in a

14

happy marriage. This is akin to what we often refer to as our conscience, and which we can more accurately refer to as the guiding Holy Spirit. He constantly guards us to protect us from wrong and to remind us that He will richly reward those who serve Him. In the same beautiful way, God has made marriage like our relationship with Him. When we are honest with God, our relationship with Him is a moment by moment, hand in His hand walk; but when we cease being honest, our relationship with Him immediately becomes strained.

Another wonderful benefit in being honest with your spouse is the peace of mind it gives, and the freedom from guilt or mistrust in each other. Don't you feel sorry for people who say, "I wouldn't trust him with a ten foot pole"? And you know why. He just can't be trusted.

I am involved frequently in family finances of clients and friends, and this takes me close to their personal lives. On one occasion when I was out of the state on an audit, the wife of one of my clients with whom I had done a lot of financial counseling called me. She was very disturbed because she felt her husband had been receiving some money and not letting her know about it. Her husband was a man who felt he should not inform his wife of any financial matters because she might not understand. So far as I know this man had not received any finances other than his ordinary income which his wife knew about. Even if he had I could not have divulged the information given to me in confidence. Here is the interesting thing: They were both leaders in their church, were Sunday school teachers and had been married many years. I don't know what all went through their marriage relationship, but it was apparent from her attitude as she talked to me that she simply didn't trust him in this area of their marriage. This distrust seriously disturbed her. A simple honest sharing of the matters of finances which actually were equally important to both of them would have brought them closer together and would have cemented their trust in each other instead of leaving a twilight zone in their mutual trust.

As a business man who works a lot in handling estate matters with widows, I would like to say, "Please, men, while you are alive, keep your wife fully informed in all the financial matters with which she will be faced if you die first."

So many women have not had the privilege of learning to handle business affairs. As a result they are left in a frustrating state of fearsome bewilderment at a time when they don't even know who to trust to advise them. (How can they trust strange men if they could not trust their own husband?) I know a lot of men who feel that their business is not any business of their wife. And I agree that it is difficult for a woman who has not been involved in the actual operation of her husband's business to become involved after he is gone. Normally it is better to have plans made while the husband is alive for a buy-out or continuation under another management so that the widow will have an income without being put into an unfair position of stepping into a situation for which she is not trained nor qualified.

I sincerely believe that the husband should set up

an appointment in an organized way with his wife at a regular recurring time just as he would call a board meeting or staff meeting of his business. He should present to her as clearly and simply as he can just how the business operates, how it is progressing, some of the major problems, how much it is making and how much of the profits must go back into the business and how much is available for the personal use of the family. He can build an enjoyable, fun time of sharing with his wife, the lover he spends so much time with while he is making a living. You see, your business is either a companion for you and your wife or it is a rival to her. I think it is wonderful for the two to love the same business instead of pulling apart by not sharing the love with whom he spends over one-third of his life.

Wives, this may be true of you if you are a business woman or work away from the home for pay. The family budget can be planned with the wife being the chairman at this same meeting. What could be more important than setting aside one evening a month to acquaint and plan such an important part of your lives together? We think it's fun.

Frances and I not only share our business affairs, but we regularly ask our seventeen-year-old daughter Joan to spend an evening with us and we keep her advised of our income and expenditures. This pleasant, willing sharing of the intimate details of our important family finances has significantly added to the trust and pleasure of our marriage and family life.

Men, I also find that when the financial report at our family directors' meeting is on the lean side, both Frances and Joan start doing everything they can to cut corners to help conserve during the financial drought. They understand our needs and want to do everything in their power to make "Poppa" happy. I'm sure because of their interest in the finances of our family, and their understanding as well, that I'm a much more enjoyable husband and father. You see, I really believe in being honest with my family in financial matters because it adds much trust, understanding and blessings to our marriage.

In the New Testament (Ephesians 4:25) we read: "Stop lying to each other; tell the truth, for we are parts of each other and when we lie to each other we are hurting ourselves."

Be Loving

by Frances

It never ceases to amaze me how the Bible relates to the current year just as well as it did back when it was written. I have never asked God to reveal the solution to any problem where I didn't discover the answer had been written many, many years ago, and yet was right for me in the twentieth century.

Ephesians 5:25-28 says, "And you husbands, show the same kind of love to your wives as Christ showed to the church when He died for her, to make her holy and clean, washed by baptism and God's Word; so that He could give her to Himself as a glorious church without a single spot or wrinkle or any other blemish, being holy and without a single fault. This is how husbands should treat their wives, loving them as parts of themselves. For since a man and his wife are now one, a man is really doing himself a favor and loving himself when he loves his wife!"

Isn't it really great that God's Word is effective and positive and real today? That is exactly how husbands should love their wives.

As Charles and I are writing this together, we'd like to speak to both of you separately and individually.

As a woman, not only do I want my husband to love me, I want him to show it! Now I don't mean any artificiality nor am I interested in any display of affection that is not sincere. But it's so thrilling to me that Charles always wants to be close to me. Since God made us one, we believe it, and act like it. We always sit next to each other, and as we are sharing our love of God with strangers, somehow or other, Charles' hand always reaches over and holds mine. Even though his mind is completely on sharing what Christ has done in our lives, this little gesture reminds me over and over again that Charles loves me in a very special way.

As we counsel with married couples, we often hear a wife complaining, "He doesn't kiss me any more." We try to find out what caused this situation to exist. It's almost always the same type of answer, "When we were first married, he wanted to kiss me while I was washing the dishes, and I told him to let me alone until I was finished!"

Girls, let me tell you, I'm never too busy to stop whatever I'm doing to kiss my husband. Often I am in the finishing stages of dinner when he gets home. When he comes into the kitchen he always asks what he can do to help. Do you know what my standard answer is? I just say, "Kiss me on the back of the neck—that's all!" And that's what he does! And never is it a source of irritation or something that slows down my getting supper. If it slows down getting supper—praise the Lord! Our love is far more special than food any day.

One of the first things that Charles learned about me was that I don't wake up real fast in the morning. I am one of those individuals who may be high octane at midnight, but in the early morning hours while trying to awake, I'm not the sharpest person in the world.

Now Charles could have done one of two things. He could have gotten mad and yelled at me as so many men do, "Can't you get your lazy body out of that bed in the morning so you can fix me a decent breakfast?" or, "I never heard of anyone so completely impossible to get out of bed. What's the matter with you?" Can you see how beautifully all our days would start off? Well, it just so happens that Charles is one of those individuals who wakes up in the morning completely wide awake! When the alarm rings, as he reaches to shut it off, his feet hit the floor and he's got it made! He runs right into the shower and if I ever peeked into the shower I'm sure I would find him having an exciting time talking to God about the great things they are planning for the day. But I have never had the courage to put my feet outside the covers as early as that.

So you see, someone like me could be a real problem to someone like Charles. But Charles asked God what to do with me to try and get me going in the morning, and God told him to treat me the same way as part of himself. Would he holler at himself and make his whole day miserable by the nasty things he had said to himself? No, of course not. He certainly would try to make his own day start off pleasantly, so do you know what he does? He kisses me! Once? Twice? No, at least three thousand times, because that's how many kisses it takes to wake me up. (At least that's how many I pretend it takes!) Now as he's kissing me with those little smothering kisses, something is happening within me. I'm beginning to realize that everything really isn't so horrible at this hour in the morning. If the day starts so pleasantly, then surely there must be other good things to wake up to, and before you know it, I've slowly but surely opened my eyes to a new day and I discover it's fabulous because we're going to spend it with God again.

I will have to let you in on a little secret, however, that I've learned. If Charles only kisses me one hundred times, and then starts for his morning shower and shave, but I think I still need more kisses to wake up, you know what I do? I make a real soft smacking sound with my lips which says to him, "Come back here and kiss me some more!" Then back he flies to me! Sometimes he wants to determine whether I'm awake or asleep so he makes a soft little smacking sound. You'd better believe, even if I'm asleep, this little love call wakes me right up and I answer him right back. Silly? Well, maybe, but it puts real thrills in our marriage, and we love it!

Love can be shown in so many ways—and as I reread the last verse of Ephesians chapter 5 I find: "And the wife must see to it that she deeply respects her husband—obeying, praising and honoring him."

Somehow or other, I think we lost a lot when they took the word "obey" out of the marriage ceremony. Don't get mad right now and stop reading, please! Let me share with you what I get from the word obey. We think of this word often as a restricting word when it really isn't. When we are married, the Bible says we become *one*. If this is truly the case how can we fail to obey ourselves? Is there anything more miserable than to be torn in two directions and not know what to do? Well, not obeying our husbands means that the *one* God made is split into two; and therefore harmony is gone.

How can we fail to do what our husbands want? Since we are part of the same one, would we not in truth, desire the same things? Obeying your husband doesn't give him the right to be your overseer, with you being the slave. Oh, no, not at all! For if that's his attitude, then he's not obeying what God says to him about treating his wife as a part of himself. So, you see, obeying isn't a bad word at all!

I think of all the movements for the so-called liberation of women. You can have them—you can take them all and put them in the ocean or wherever you want to, because I don't want to be liberated. I want my man to protect me, love me, cherish me and take care of me the rest of my life.

And then the Bible says, "Praising and honoring him." I love to tell the world about my husband—not only about the man Charles Hunter, but especially about him as the follower of Christ. Not all of us have the opportunity of telling the world about our husbands. But you know, I love to talk in praise of him right to his face! I thank God, right while Charles is listening to my prayers, for giving him to me. I constantly am thanking Charles for all the wonderful little things he does for me. (I have a feeling he enjoys knowing that I appreciate all he does for me.)

Honor him? Yes, I do. I honor his right for privacy if and when he wants it. I honor his right to have me by his side at all times. I honor his right to have me love him all the days of my life. I honor his right to put his head on my shoulder when he's tired. I honor his right to want his home clean and shiny. I honor his right to have his clothes clean and in his closet where they belong at all times. I honor his right to live within our means and not cause him worry about finances if I can help it. I honor his right to share with me the innermost secrets of his soul, knowing that I will keep these secrets within the walls of my heart, never to be shared with anyone. I honor his right to have me waiting as his haven of rest when he's worked hard all day at the office. I honor his right to expect me to be his wife at all times.

Do you know why? Because I *love* him—and I want him to know it.

by Charles

As I have let my mind float hundreds of hours back and forth through the New Testament, I find an ever increasing depth to the use and meaning of *love*. I find that it is the strongest, most powerful word used in the Bible because it is even used to encompass God Himself when it says, "God is love." When you try to describe God, it always reverts to "love."

Now since God is love, He wants the very best for His children. God knows how much every human being needs love, so He created woman for man. "Then the Lord God said, 'It is not good that the man should be alone; I will make a helpmeet suitable for him'" (Genesis 2:7,18). Surely, God in His infinite wisdom knew how much I needed love and how much I needed to love someone special. So He gave Frances to me. Since wives are given by God to man, we should put our wives before all else in the world except before God and His Son, Christ Jesus. Because this is the way God intended it to be, it is easy for me to put my wife before my business, friends, sports, or anything else that might hold my interest.

How can our partner know we're loving or in love

if we don't act like it? And, also, if we don't mention the subject occasionally? One of the most important highlights of my day is my return home at night. I always call Frances if it's possible at all, to find out if there is anything she needs from the store that I can pick up, and to let her know that I'm anxious to get home to her. No man feels more like a king than I do when I drive into our driveway. Frances is always dressed like she is going to a party when I arrive home—her dress, hair, makeup, perfume, everything is just as though she were going right out the door. But the exciting thing is the fact that *it's for me* she has done all this.

The minute the car drives up in the driveway, she's at the door with her arms outstretched waiting for me to run into them, and she's all puckered up for me to kiss her. I don't have to ask her if it's all right to kiss her and mess up her makeup. I don't have to wonder if she's in the mood to kiss me. I *know* by her loving actions and her eagerness to be at the door when I get there. And what do I do? I jump out of the car as quickly as I can and run as fast as my legs will carry me, because the minute the motor stops and I open the car door, I hear a smacking sound of kisses already reaching my ears and urging me to run into her arms where I know the sounds become loving kisses on my lips. Then her arms squeeze me so tightly I just melt into them and my work-day has ended in a perfectly beautiful way. My evening at home has started with love expressed so very dramatically my heart just about bursts out of my chest. Is that any way to greet a husband? You bet it is!

I think of a couple I have known who had a great love for each other and had an almost perfect marriage. One thing, though, that was missing was the lack of "expressed" love by the wife. She did everything she thought she could to please her husband and show him a kind of love. But she almost never told her husband she loved him and never showed the love in a personal way such as a hug, kiss or caress. How much better their marriage would be if she would only express her love in some personal, intimate way.

Frances has described our "smacking love calls," and I would like to add just one little thing she does that thrills me to the very bone. When my work load demands extra time, I prefer getting up early and going to the office rather than working late in the evening. To leave for work without kissing Frances even a few times just isn't possible. When she is asleep and I'm dressed and ready for work, I tiptoe to her bedside and whisper in her ear, "Don't wake up, just let me kiss you." After a few gentle kisses, I softly say good-bye. But before I can get away, I always receive an abundant supply of returned kisses from the most thrilling girl in the world. If women would just learn to make their man feel like a man, it's amazing what would happen to their marriages. If they prized the kisses of their husband, it's amazing how many more they would get. When a woman lets her man KNOW he's a man, he'll do anything in the world for her.

The *little* things are what make a marriage exciting. Recently I was working in a place where it was very inconvenient to go out for lunch and so

Frances made a lunch which was very good. But the very best part of it was a little note tucked inside the napkin which simply said, "I love you, Sweetheart." The second day when I opened my lunch there was another little note which said, "I love you more today than yesterday."

Frances frequently leaves little notes where and when I least expect to find them. Let me share one she just left on my pillow under the bedspread when she left for a nine-day tour (which we hope is the last one of any length I will not get to accompany her). When I went to bed the first night after she left, I was welcomed by the beautiful, familiar aroma of her favorite perfume. She had sprayed my pillow lightly with it just before she left—WOW! The funny thing is I didn't discover the note until the next morning, but this is what it said:

"Dearest Charles:

Well, my Tiger, I'm off again—and while right now it seems like such a long time, I know it will go by quickly, because God doesn't want us to suffer away from each other and long for each other. So every night when you lay your head down on this pillow, just remember I love you with all my heart, mind, body and soul, and I'm so glad God made you mine. I'm so glad that somehow in His great wisdom He knew we needed each other. Even though I'm gone now, I need you every single moment, and you are there, in my heart and in my mind all the time.

I've even sprayed the pillow case with my perfume, just to remind you that I'm not so far away,

29

as long as I am in your thoughts. Time to run, my
love, but I did want you to know that
                    I LOVE YOU
                    I LOVE YOU
                    I LOVE YOU
                    Your Woman,
                    Frances."
Wouldn't that letter do something to any man
whose wife wrote it to him? You'd better believe it
intensified my love for Frances, because of her concern about my welfare while she had to be gone.
Since she is a fast typist, I'm sure the note didn't
take her longer than two or three minutes to type. It
wasn't the time involved, but the thought and love
which prompted it that made it mean so very much
to me. These little things have a way of keeping and
making a marriage exciting.

I have a great love for counseling with individuals about their needs and in letting God's Holy
Spirit direct in guiding them into a closer walk with
Jesus and thereby into a more enjoyable and happy
life. One of the frequent complaints made to me is
by women who have been active in church work for
all their lives and whose husbands will not go to
church and will not even listen to them when they
try to get them to become Christians. The husbands
seem to have little interest in them anymore and because there is such a vast difference in their activities, the husbands find little in common with the
wives.

A husband often gets so involved in his work that
he spends very little time with his wife. Too often
he begins drinking and then, to the wife's dismay,

she suspects he is out with other women. Or more often he comes home, eats and sits in front of the TV all evening. Then the wife asks me to counsel with her about what to do and asks for prayer.

Do you know what my answer usually is? I ask the wife how much love and affection she has shown her husband. How long has it been since she showed truly feminine love to her husband? This usually brings a sudden, shocking reflection of the many past years of her life and she sees she has not made it really attractive and desirous for her husband to want to rush into her arms.

About the same time she is looking into this personal mirror she realizes that her husband probably has been looking for a vision of Christ in someone. Because his wife has been such a pious church member, he thinks that she certainly must be the real place to look. But if the wife does not show love—for God *is* love—then she does not show God. So, the husband figures, if God is *without love,* like his wife, why should he go to church? Or, why look further for the God who left his wife so lacking in affection?

I feel sure most men are a lot like me. They have a great need and desire to be loved and are looking for some way to satisfy this longing. A good moral man is likely to involve himself in work as a respectable solution to avoid the pull that hits his heart when he wants so very much to be loved and can't find it at home. He can't believe it is to be found in Jesus because he cannot see Christ in his religious wife who doesn't have love or joy. So he is turned off at home and in church.

Love is shown in a thousand *little* ways. Those fewer big ways are not quite as important. Think of the times you could have met your husband at the door looking your best, hugged him and kissed him, let him smell a little fresh perfume you applied as you freshened yourself for the one most important in your life.

It only takes a little while to listen to him tell you what has been on his mind at the office, shop or store or wherever he works. Your welcome listening ear will make him feel better about the bad things of the day and proud of the accomplishments. For in this sharing he is making you a vital part of his life. Then, as you share the events of your day, he will become more and more eager to listen. In these ways you become one in activities instead of being two disinterested and apart individuals for about ten hours of your day. I think we can safely say, "Love without ceasing," just as the Bible says, "Pray without ceasing."

Try to think of little things you can do for your husband tonight when he comes home. It may shock him at first, so go kind of gentle. But within a short time you will be amazed at how he has been catching up on his work earlier and earlier and is able to get home sooner.

I can't wait to get off work and rush home to Frances. God must make a list of little things for her to think of to make me thrilled and happy to be with her.

By the way, men, I hope you have been listening while I talked to the ladies because it's exciting and rewarding to do lots of little things for our wives.

They need love and affection shown in a thousand little ways. And as we make an effort to please them, they will just think we are perfect lovers as we sweep them off their feet. The drawing to our wives or husbands should not be unlike the drawing we feel toward God because it is actually the same kind of love God created within us to demonstrate His love in a way we can understand.

Can you see why I love Frances so dearly and want to be with her every minute of my life and never tire of her? She constantly lets her love flow outward to others and I am so very blessed to be in the center of her river of love.

When Jesus said it is better to give than to receive He surely meant love. The only way we can receive love is to willingly, longingly, anxiously give all of our love freely without thought of receiving it in return, whether we are speaking of love to our wife or to our Christ and our God. We must want God and Christ Jesus more than anything in our lives before we can even approach the love God wants us to give. But when we find the secret of releasing all our love to Him without any reservation, then and only then can God return that love along with the abundant blessings He promises and gives to us.

In the same wonderful way, when we love our companion through Christ we must want our beloved companion more than anything in our lives except God and our Lord Jesus. I am convinced that love can only be perfect in marriage when your love passes through God to your spouse.

We have both shared how we feel about being

loving, and we hope you have gotten the idea that we believe not only in being loving, but letting each other know how much we love!

Be Patient

by Frances

What a beautiful virtue this is. Isn't it a good thing that God is patient with us? Can you imagine how much His patience must have been tried when you were first added to His family? Can you imagine how He must have felt when you kept falling back, and then scrambling to grab His hand again, only to turn loose of it again in your search for the things of the world? Do you have any idea of the patience God must have had to put up with—well maybe not you, but certainly me? When I think that His patience lasted for forty-nine years before I finally began to see a glimmer of light, I realize more and more what a virtue patience is. Suppose He had gotten tired and said disgustedly, "Oh, well, she'll never learn. She will never get the message." What would have happened? I would still be out there in the darkness of sin.

Since we were made in the image of God surely we can hope for some of the same virtues, and patience is one. When we first get married we are on such a cloud we close our eyes to the faults of the other. But when the honeymoon is over, we come back to earth again. It's the same thing as when we became Christians and we started living in the world again. The bubble broke and we really began to wonder. . . . Then as we did the things God told us to do—reading the Bible and praying, the excitement came back again. And the same situation applies to marriage. When we begin to look at each other twenty-four hours a day, sometimes we can get discouraged, but remember, if God put you together, there's certainly a solution to your problems. Just have patience.

It's a good thing Charles has the beautiful patience of a saint. I am, by nature, much more rambunctious and impetuous than Charles is. It just isn't in me to carefully, patiently plan things the way he does.

Another one of my great "unattributes" is my inability to back a car up the way it should be backed up. I am all right on a straight road, but the driveway out of our yard is as crooked as a snake. It's the kind you have to back out unless you can turn the car around in an area that wasn't designed to turn a car around in. Even when the car is sitting in front of the door, which leaves only a small crooked area to back out, I usually run over the grass on both sides, knock down the little metal sign that has our address on it, and generally create havoc before I end up on the street.

Does Charles yell and criticize me for this? No, he doesn't! First of all, I admit that I am not a good, crooked backer-upper and when I confess it, he forgives me. He even forgives me for knocking the sign down. This has taken great patience on the part of Charles. Do you realize how irritated he could get at me? In his patient, kind way, when one of the cars is left home for me, he turns it around in the driveway and points the nose toward the street, and then I have no trouble. Do you know why he is so patient? Because he's made in the image of God. I'm sure his patience will go on and on and on, and I'll keep trying to learn how to back up "crooked."

First Corinthians 13:4 says, "Love is patient and kind." Not only patient, *but kind*. Sometimes we might pretend to be patient, but the remarks could be cutting instead of kind.

I cooked on an electric stove for many years before Charles and I were married. When I got to Houston I discovered we had a gas stove which cooks a lot differently than an electric one. Right off the bat I burned a hole in the teakettle. Now that I think about it, it wasn't the fault of the stove, but it was my absentmindedness because I forgot to turn the flame off. Shortly after that I cremated a pan with some eggs in it. They were supposed to be hard-boiled, but that was hardly the word for them. When I finally smelled the smoke which came surging through the house, the pan had melted on the stove. And lying there, looking me right in the eye, were four black little eggs.

I said my usual "Praise the Lord, anyway!" and tried to air out the house. Just about this time, Charles came home. I didn't try to hide what had happened because that's not being honest. I told Charles what I had done and we laughed as we put the remains of the eggs down the garbage disposal. This situation could have ended up with all kinds of problems were it not for the fact that Charles is patient and kind. Patient, because he puts up with me; and kind, because he never says anything about it. He doesn't harbor grudges, either, because he believes I'll learn (eventually).

Charles acquired a teen-age daughter when he married me. We had a crying good time recently as we all stood in court and she legally became his daughter. How would you like to acquire a teen-ager when you had never had children in your previous marriage? How would you have handled a sixteen-year-old girl?

Joan got to Texas on the 22nd of January. I had to leave on tour on the 24th of January. It's a good thing they both had patience and kindness, because here were two complete strangers living in the same house, who were supposed to be father and daughter just because mama married Charles. Here is Joan in a new city, a new state, a new house, a new school, a new church, a new daddy, and can you imagine how she feels?

And then here's daddy, a C.P.A. right in the heart of income tax time, and he discovers that Joan's Florida driver's license isn't valid in Texas unless she takes driving lessons. Mama is out of town, so Charles had to take Joan to school every day, pick her up after school and then every night he had to take her over to driving school so she could get her Texas license.

He was getting up at 5:30 in the morning to get started on his work, then having to return home in order to get Joan to school at 8 o'clock, then run back to his office or whatever client's office he was in, and keep an eye on the clock so he could pick her up when school was out. It was a real hectic schedule for him, but he didn't complain one single time. Charles certainly exerted tremendous patience during this time. Such a schedule day after day can be a real drain on one's energy, patience and love.

And while we're on the subject of Joan, I can't help but mention the fact that one of the contributing reasons to the sweetness of our marriage is Charles' attitude toward Joan. So many men marry women who have children from a previous marriage, and fail to recognize the fact that the children do exist and must be loved as much as they would love their very own. So many marriages end up on shaky ground because people do not sit down and intelligently discuss the treatment of their children. While children are certainly beautiful gifts from God, they can also create some of the biggest hazards in marriage if we don't exercise patience.

Many times a lack of patience is a lack of accepting our mate for what he or she is. So many people make the mistake of thinking they are going to change their mate after they are married. What they are really saying is, "I'm going to have MY own way all the time after we're married, because I'M going to change *him*." As a result we don't let little things really irritate us before we're married, thinking we'll change them after marriage. But when we wake up in the daylight of marriage, we discover the little things which we thought we would change are still there and we begin to get irritated.

We forget that the only person who is able to

change another's disposition is Jesus Christ Himself. If we are truly one as the Bible says, we are letting our left hand become annoyed with our right hand, and letting our left hand say, "I'm going to cut you off because I don't like you." If we would just accept our mates for the reasons we married them and learn to adjust in harmony with each other to the differences we might have, we would discover marriage could be a lot more exciting.

Why don't you make a little list right now of the things that irritate you about your spouse, and see if they didn't exist before you were married? Then try exercising a little more patience instead of irritation. And then be honest with yourself. Ask yourself, "Is there a real reason for my irritation, or should I be more patient and kind?"

Did it ever dawn on you that love, understanding and patience can do more to change undesirable characteristics than anything else? God removes the things from our lives that are not pleasing in His sight through His great love of us. When we find ourselves totally committed to Him, we want to please Him. In wanting to please Him, the things which we know displease Him fall by the wayside. The same principle is true of a husband-wife relationship. If we exhibit patience in loving our mates, and our love is unchanging in spite of their idiosyncrasies, they will want to change because of our patience and love. Try it on your mate and see what happens.

Be Courteous

by Frances

"Love is . . . never haughty or selfish or rude" (1 Corinthians 13:4,5).

That's what the Bible says! And how many times do we ignore being courteous to the ones we love the most or at least the ones we are supposed to love the most. Do you ladies give your husband the privilege of opening the car door for you, or do you madly rush out of the house, open the car door and plunk yourself in the car before he can even catch you? Or maybe you fool around so long he disgustedly gets in the car ahead of you and is impatiently waiting for you to come out.

I'm so glad that early in our marriage God put into my mind the idea of letting Charles be a gentleman. And oftentimes, it's *our* fault, you know, that our men are not gentlemen.

Two days after we were married in Miami, we drove the 1,200 miles to our home in Houston which I had never seen. We drove into the yard and around the driveway. Charles stopped the car, got out, opened the gates, got back into the car, drove the car ahead, stopped, got out, shut the gates, got back into the car and drove it into the garage. Then he got out and came around on my side of the car and opened the door. This was just perfect, because I felt so utterly feminine and loved and protected, and Charles felt so masculine and protective.

Then came the second day I was in my new home. We went out and did a little shopping and when we came back I flipped out of the car real quickly and opened the one side of the gate. Then as I turned to walk to open the other side, I looked at Charles who had gotten out of the car to open them. He was crushed! His mouth didn't say a word, but his face said, "Honey, I want to take care of you. Won't you let me be a gentleman?"

Would you like for me to tell you what I did? I walked right over to the gate I had opened, I didn't say a word to Charles, but I shut it, and then I ran back to the car, got in, shut the car door and sat there as feminine as anything you ever saw. Charles got the message. He straightened his shoulders, opened both gates, drove the car through, got out, shut the gates, drove into the garage, opened the door for me and let me out and almost broke my ribs as he hugged me.

And I hope you are interested in knowing that I have never opened the car door since that day and I never intend to. I wouldn't deprive my beloved husband of one of the greatest privileges a man has—that of being the strong one in the family.

The Bible says, "Love is not selfish or rude." And how rude can a wife be when she doesn't let her husband be the gentleman he wants to be? On the other hand, how rude can a husband be when he doesn't show enough love for his wife to be concerned as to whether or not she even gets in the car when they are going someplace?

Charles always treats me like a precious flower and he doesn't want the petals to get crushed— AND I LOVE IT. And it's amazing how many people notice the way he treats me.

Not long ago we had returned from a tour and stopped at a local store which is next door to the cleaners. Charles said, "Do you mind if I go to the cleaners while you're at the store?" I said, "No, honey, that's O.K." So he got out of the car, opened the door and helped me out. He held my arm as we walked to the door of the store where he opened the door; then said, "I'll be back in just a couple of minutes, soon as I get the cleaning." This is perfectly normal with us at all times.

As I went to the counter, there was a young man about eighteen or nineteen years of age who looked at me very puzzled and said, "Is that your old man?"

I laughed and said, "That's my husband if that's what you mean."

Then he said, "I don't believe it. People just don't act like that anymore. Does he do that all the time?"

I said, "Sure, he does that all the time." And the kid looked utterly amazed because he couldn't believe that married people still treated each other like that.

About three weeks later we went in the same 7-11 Store. The young man was working again and when Charles opened the door for me, he said, "Here come the lovers!" Then he added, "He's still opening the door for you. That's really cool!"

The next time I went in my daughter was with me instead of my husband, and the young man said, "Where's the old man?" I told him he was at work, and he turned to the girl working with him and said, "That's the one—the one whose old man opens the car door for her all the time."

Just the other day we went in the store and a new girl said, "Are you the one whose husband always opens the car door?" Look at the chain reaction caused by the fact that my husband is a gentleman, and I let him be one!

Sometimes we think it's fun to joke or kid in a critical manner, but may I say this is equal to taking a dose of marital poison if you're not careful? What may sound funny today might not sound half so funny a year from today. Two years from today the same critical comment might end up as grounds for divorce.

I've heard couples affectionately call each other pet names and in a few years the pet became a tiger with nasty claws. An in-the-beginning loving remark such as, "Frances is such a slob, but I love her anyway," could turn out to be a nasty cutting remark, "You slob, can't you ever keep this house clean?" before the end of a year was out. By the end of the second year, instead of being called by name, you might end up being called just, "Hey, slob!" It might sound funny the first time, but let me assure you these kinds of things do not sound nearly as funny as marriage wears on.

I have heard women tell things about their husbands that might have been laughable at that instant, but which I'm sure cut their husbands to the quick. Sometimes these involve situations where we are not at our best for a moment. The other partner should never rejoice at a cutting, hurting situation. Because when God made us one, when something hurts one of us, it should automatically hurt the two of us, since we are actually *one*.

I am recalling a man whose wife made a mistake in their checkbook (who hasn't?) and he made a statement in public that "She is so stupid she couldn't even add two and two." Over the years his comments about her stupidity continued until she was thoroughly convinced that she was stupid and could never hope to be anything else. She almost ended up in a mental institution just because of a cutting remark which sounded funny the first time it was said, but got to be a monster in their marriage. (For the records, they are now divorced because of her "stupidity"—and he married another "stupid" woman.)

Is this what God calls us for? He says love does not rejoice at wrong, but rejoices in the right. And believe it or not, this comes under the heading of courtesy. Isn't it common courtesy to our mates to rejoice in their accomplishments, and sorrow with them when something goes wrong? If we are truly *one* how can it be otherwise?

Sometimes situations occur where one partner is put in a position of being more outstanding, clever, talented or witty than the other. The attention of the world (meaning your friends and neighbors) is turned completely on the one outstanding partner. What happens to the other partner? Does the one partner rejoice because he is getting all the attention or does he bring out the outstanding qualities of his not so outstanding partner? I have seen couples do this, and it thrills me to death. I love these truly outstanding men who constantly mention the tremendous qualities of their wives. Love doesn't rejoice at one partner being submerged while the other one rises up. Love rejoices when two people, because they are one, rise together.

by Charles

"In response to all He has done for us, let us outdo each other in being helpful and kind to each other and in doing good." That's what is said about courtesy in Hebrews 10:24.

Somewhere I have read that God created us with a desire to do good and I feel that within all men there is a basic desire to do good which is really significantly expressed in being courteous to those we love. I know I have a built-in desire to be courteous at every opportunity and I don't feel that I am a bit different than any other average man. Being courteous is just simply being loving. God said to love our wife or husband. He even went so far as to command us to love our neighbors; and then further, even to love the unlovely.

How can we show love without showing courtesy? Courtesy is expressed in the form of good manners, and to have good manners we should strive to learn ways to express this to others.

In Luke 14:26 are listed the most precious possessions known to man: "Anyone who wants to be My follower must love Me far more than he does his own father, mother, wife, children, brothers, or sisters—yes, more than his own life—otherwise he cannot be My disciple." Next to Christ Himself my wife is the most precious pearl that exists and I want to cherish, polish, protect and love that pearl of great price. Never do I want to treat her with anything short of my very best, which includes every courtesy I can find to give her. For the men here are just a few little courtesies which lift up your wife when you exercise them enthusiastically, in love, and just because you want to:

How about being as regular as possible in the time you come home from work at night? Or calling before you leave? Or if you are going to be late, giving her a short call?

How about jotting in your date book or making a note somewhere that will not let you forget an important date or event meaningful to her?

How about thinking twice—before you buy a new set of golf clubs, or new fishing tackle—what could this be used for if I spent this on something she would like?

How about keeping your promise when you say, "I'll take next Saturday off and we will go on a picnic or go shopping together"?

Keep from letting other things or people, except in unusual circumstances, from becoming more important than the one who means most in your life?

How about just being consistent by telling her in words and actions that you love her more than anything else in this world?

How about shaving and putting on your best aftershave lotion and sharpening up your looks on your day off so she can see you at your best, even if your best that day calls for work clothes?

Be courteous and do the things she wants done

around the house which you put off because you are too busy.

How about taking her out often if she likes to do that and treating her like the most important lady in your world?

How about volunteering to take her shopping, or suggesting in the middle of the year that you get something special just for her?

How about asking her what she would like to do some evening, instead of spending the whole evening reading the paper or watching TV?

How about giving her a hand with the children without complaining—and doing it *all* the time?

How about always opening the car door and seeing to it that she's inside before you walk around and get in? And how about always opening the car door and letting her out of the car?

For the Women

How about not interrupting him when he's talking, even if you think you can tell the story better than he can?

How about fixing his favorite dinner tonight with all the little extras he enjoys to go along with it?

How about spending a whole day cleaning up the spare bedroom which is always a mess?

Jesus came to be a servant. How about waiting on your husband for all his wants and desires for a week? Then see how much longer you'll want to do just that.

How about staying off the telephone around the supper hour so he can call you and let you know when he's coming home?

How about restricting your telephone calls to a few minutes at night when he's home? If you have a lot to say to a friend, call her back in the morning.

How about getting rid of that pile of unironed clothes, or putting away all the washing?

How about taking time out right now to do the little mending jobs he's asked you to do on his clothes?

How about putting your husband first before your children—and letting him know he comes first?

How about having a good listening ear when he comes home from work?

How about pouring your love into your husband instead of giving too much of it to your children—or grandchildren?

Be Considerate

by Frances

Every single consideration in this book goes right back to what the Bible says. "Love does not demand its own way." In other words, be considerate of your partner. And marriage is always a two-way street. Consideration is necessary on the part of both persons.

Charles and I found out even before we were married, that both of us love to give. In learning this secret, we learned that the secret of living is giving.

Put the desires of your mate *first*. It isn't important to me what I do, but it is important to me that the desires of Charles' heart be satisfied. By the same token, he feels the same way, and it makes every situation so much easier to handle as it comes up. Here are some of the little things that came up early in our marriage, and which were quickly resolved because we put the wishes of the other one first.

I have never been the world's greatest housekeeper. As a matter of fact, I might win a prize for being a miserable one. For many years I excused myself for I reasoned that I worked so much I just didn't have time to take care of the housework.

Anyway, the dirt would be there long after I was gone. Charles' favorite verse at that time was, "You are dust, and to dust you shall return" (Genesis 3:19). I remember how many times I have jumped out of bed in the morning, gotten dressed to go to work and said to myself, "I'll let the bed air out today, because I don't like to make it up right away." Then when I got home that night I would say, "There's no point in making up the bed now because it's almost time to go to bed." So the only time the bed got made was when the maid came on Friday and changed the sheets!

Frankly, I don't like housework. For years I've said I never did like it. And for years I said I never would! But do you know what I discovered? Charles likes the house immaculate at all times! Ugh . . . what was I going to do? Was I going to maintain my individuality and say, "I've never been a good housekeeper and I never will be"? You had better believe I did not. I said, "Lord, you know how much I hate housework, so would you please put a desire in my heart to want to keep this house clean?" And then I added, "And Lord, would you please show me how to do the job efficiently and quickly, because you know how much I love Charles and how I want to please him."

Now, it didn't all happen at one time. First, God put a broom in my hand. Then little by little God began to show me how to keep the house immaculate at all times. With no feeling or pressure at all, I discovered it is just as easy to make the bed quickly as it is several hours later.

I also discovered that it's much easier to keep all

your cosmetics neat and tidy than it is to let them get in a big mess on the counter in the bathroom. I have learned as I use each item of cosmetics to put it immediately back where it belongs. I've learned to take about three seconds, when I leave the bathroom after dressing, to make sure that nothing is left in there to detract from the attractiveness of the room. It takes two more seconds to make sure that everything is where it should be.

I also have learned to instantly put my shoes away when I take them off instead of letting them sit in the middle of the room to be picked up (maybe) at a later time. I've also learned that when I take off my bedroom slippers I can immediately slip them into the closet where they belong, instead of letting them sit somewhere else.

I have also learned to fold clothes the minute they come out of the dryer and put them away right then. I've also learned to get up from the table and *instantly* put the dishes in the dishwasher, clean up the sink, stove, etc. I've also discovered the secret of picking up things that accidentally get put down, and returning them to their proper place. Even more important, I've learned *not* to put them down accidentally, but to put things where they belong right off the bat.

I have learned to do things instantly instead of putting them off because I don't like to do them. It's amazing how much fresher and cleaner your mind is when it is not all bogged down with things you have to do, but hate to do.

I have also learned how to get the meals ready without creating havoc in the kitchen. (Ask God to teach you the same thing. It's amazing how many businesses He is in.) I have learned how to sit down at the dinner table and have the kitchen look as though I had not cooked a single thing.

As a matter of fact, when I get up in the morning, the first thing I ask God after our initial greeting is to really help me fly through my morning chores, so I can be ready to face the world at a reasonable hour with all my little duties behind me. And of course, since I always ask the Lord what we ought to have for dinner, I don't have to spend a lot of time thinking about that. Because my time is at such a premium, and because we live quite a distance from the store, I do my grocery shopping once a week and save both time and money on car expenses by shopping this way. It's amazing how much more time you have for everything when you do this—plus the fact, it pleases my husband when things run efficiently. And I've discovered that keeping house is fun besides.

There are so many little areas where consideration can be shown if we would just take time to realize it. One of the things I think is very important is to be dressed when my husband comes home. After a man is out in the business world all day, if he comes home to a wife who looks like she has had the same clothes on for a week, it's not the most appealing sight in the world.

When I know it's close to "Charles" time, I always check my makeup to be sure I look fresh and clean. I take a good look at my hair to make sure it's in good shape. Above all else, I make sure that whatever outfit I have on looks right. When I greet him at the door, if I have had an apron on, I quickly take off the apron so that he sees me at my best when he gets the first glimpse of me after a day at the office. Maybe he doesn't even notice it, but I have fresh cologne or perfume on when he comes home too, because I want him to have something interesting waiting for him.

Often when I counsel, women complain about the fact that their husbands don't come home from work as fast as they could and I always ask them, "What do they have to come home to? Is it interesting and appealing, exciting and responsive?" The reason men don't hurry home from work is often because they don't like what's waiting for them there. And I certainly wouldn't like to hurry home to a wife who hasn't dressed up to look her very best for me, if I were a man.

Charles does so many little things to show his consideration for me that I find it hard to list them all.

Because I'm on my feet so much of the time, I wear special nurses' shoes which have to be tied. Believe it or not, my darling husband always keeps my shoes polished sparkling white and when I put them on each day, he ties them! This is only a little thing, but it's a very special thing to me, not because I can't tie my own shoes, but because I know he's not thinking he's too good to do it. In that moment when he kneels to tie my shoes, he says, "I love you" more than words could ever say—It shows me there isn't anything in the world he wouldn't do for me. If men would just learn to realize how much these little, loving gestures mean to their wives! And now I'll let you in on a secret, girls. When Charles bends over to tie my shoes, I always plant a big smack on his bald head.

I forgot to mention what Charles does in the kitchen. Many men think they're too masculine to help in the kitchen because that's a woman's work. Charles discovered that because we are *one* it's not sissified to be in the kitchen with me when we get ready to clear the table after supper. He doesn't feel he's too good to quickly rinse the dishes off and help me get out of the kitchen, because he doesn't like to spend time away from me. We have some of our most exciting discussion about the day's activities as we clear the dishes and clean the kitchen for the night. It gives me more time to spend with him during the evening, doing the things we like to do together.

Charles is always considerate of my physical condition. If he thinks I'm tired, he sees to it that I get to bed early, and he makes sure that nothing will disturb me if I happen to be overly-tired and need additional sleep. He doesn't hesitate to take the spread off the bed if he gets into the bedroom first, and neither do I. Because he is the early riser in our family, he sees to it that he's in and out of the shower before I am ready to get in. Charles does not expect me to be his personal maid who runs after him cleaning up the mess he makes. When he finishes showering and shaving, the bathroom is immaculate and not a mess for me to clean up. So many times, these little things are the source of the greatest irritation unless we approach them all in a positive vein.

Well, now, how about the top of the toothpaste tube? Does he leave it off, and do you do a slow burn because of it? Or does she leave it off, and then when you go to use it the next morning, there's some trace of her rouge right across the end of the tube? Sometimes these little irritations of life can be easily solved by learning to put the top on the toothpaste. That's really not a major project if you love your spouse enough. And rather than have endless fights about it, why not buy two tubes? And then one of you can be a slob and the other one doesn't have to worry about it. I know a couple who almost got a divorce because she was so irritated by his leaving the top off the toothpaste.

Does he take off his clothes and drop them right there and expect you to pick them up? Well, one of two things can happen. You can pick them up and love it and charge it off to one of his endearing little habits, or he might discover (like I did) that it's much easier and more considerate to hang them up when he takes them off, or to put them in the dirty clothes hamper. While both Charles and I maintain our own individual personalities, we believe that because God made us *one*, we should act like it and never let our marriage get lopsided.

Charles happens to like for me to go to bed when he goes to bed. Maybe he has had a harder day at the office than I have had at home. Maybe I got to sleep a couple of winks longer in the morning than he did, and I'm not really ready to go to bed. But I know that Charles wants me at his side when he goes to bed, so do you know what I do? I go to bed. Now if I don't get to sleep quite as fast as he does, I spend the rest of the time praying and talking to God and just meditating, but I'm right where I should be—alongside my husband. Many wives sit up late watching TV. Many marriages would be a lot more exciting if the wives realized that their husbands like to have them beside them when they go to bed.

How about the groceries when you go to the store? Charles always carries them into the house. Not that I am not capable, but he's stronger than I am, and lots of times the bags are heavy. It's just a little thing, but as I have indicated, it's the little things that really count up.

And here's a good subject—*money!* Are you really considerate of the way you spend your money? Most men work hard and when they find their wives spending it foolishly, it doesn't set well with them. Girls, we could all take a few lessons in how to spend more wisely the money our husbands earn.

Did you ever think about asking God before you make a purchase? It's amazing how good a job He can do with your money, and how He can curb that unnecessary spending. Like all women, I like to buy something unnecessary once in a while, but I've learned that if I say, "God, is this necessary?" God really answers me real quick. I've saved a lot of money this way. God will provide our every need—the Bible says so, but God doesn't say He will provide for all our foolish spending. Let's start depending on Him a little more, shall we?

Since my beloved husband is a C.P.A. he has a much more orderly mind than I have. And one of the things I found out was the fact he likes to be on time. We have had a lot of give and take in our marriage and we have both learned to do a lot of things differently than we used to. Where I used to fly around at the last minute hectically getting ready to catch a plane, I discovered this could be a great source of irritation to Charles. So I just manage to get things organized a little bit better and we have been getting to the airport a half hour early these days. Because God made us one, we should have a oneness in desires. But again it's a question of whether we think we should maintain our individuality or whether we are really trying to make marriage what God intended for it to be.

And heaven help the working man from coming home to a perpetual griper. There isn't anything worse to greet a man when he comes home from work than a woman who gripes about all the terrible things that happened during the day. If you have a gripe to make, wait until his tummy is full of a good dinner you have prepared, and then make it in love. But give him a chance to get away from the problems of his business life when he gets home, without having to dread the first sentence you're going to say because it's a negative idea.

God says not to worry about the "cares of life," and if you will make your marriage positive it's amazing how the negative things will quickly disappear. What good is it going to do if you gripe because the garbage men didn't take the trash today? Is that going to make your marriage more successful? Is all the griping in the world going to remove that trash before the men come around again? Is it going to make your marriage more exciting and glamorous? Is it going to give you more time to grow up in Christ? Little daily irritations like griping can become a tool of the devil to keep you from talking about the things that will make your marriage loving and exciting.

Well, now, I wonder what Charles is going to say on this subject! After reading what I said about him, I'm convinced he's the considerate one in our house, and I wonder what he's going to find to say about what I do to show him consideration!

by Charles

We were discussing at church recently what it means to be totally dedicated to Jesus Christ. I love the way it is stated in Luke 14:26,33: "If anyone comes to Me, and does not hate his own father and mother and wife and children and brothers and sisters, yes, and even his own life, he cannot be My disciple. . . . So therefore, no one of you can be My disciple who does not give up all his own possessions."

When God's Holy Spirit first showed me the meaning of this, I was (and still am) searching for every way I could find to release all of my life to Christ for His full and complete control. I read and reread this Scripture and asked God to reveal its full meaning to me. Then it came through loud and clear. I first realized that the things Jesus named (our family) are the most prized earthly possessions we can have. Then I wondered why He said we must hate them. So I asked God again what He meant and quickly it came to me that the greatest distance between any two points is the distance between love and hate. This meant that all Christ was asking of me was to love Him more than my greatest possession—that my love for Him had to be as far above my love for Frances as love was from hate.

What does all of this have to do with keeping our marriage exciting? It is marvelous how we can have a greater love for our wife or husband if this love first flows through Christ. This makes it a pure, healthy, wonderful love and it makes it possible to love our mate with all our heart, mind, soul and body and at the same time love our Lord the same way, only to a greater degree. So if we put our wife first in all of our lives, *through Christ*, then we will be eager to be considerate of all her desires. I think it's marvelous how God arranged for us to love Him most and still let us love our mates most, too!

At the time I am writing this chapter, Frances is twelve-hundred miles away on a nine-day tour, one of the few times where God has not allowed me to accompany her. Because I had taken my eyes off of Christ and put them on myself, I was feeling sorry for myself that I was not along with her, sharing in the excitement of her trip.

One of the things about Frances that I appreciate the most is her consideration of my feelings, and her concern for me when she can see that I am not up where I should be. She always calls me when she has to be away, and even if it is between planes, she phones me just for a few minutes to let me know she loves me. Just the fact that she is on the lookout for telephone booths lets me know that she is thinking about me. And she always calls me the last thing at night before she goes to bed.

Well, she called, and it didn't take her much time

to detect the loneliness in my voice and words. Also it didn't take me long to confess to her about my depressed feeling. Even though it was late at night and she needed sleep, she took the last ounce of her energy and pumped it into me and made me feel so completely loved. I spent the next day and night putting my eyes back on Jesus and taking them off myself.

Frances was concerned about my depressed feeling, and even though we had discussed before she left that we would try to hold our daily calls down to a reasonable length, she knew how important it was to me to have time with her on the telephone, to talk, to pray, to love. She called me Saturday afternoon to talk for a few moments. Saturday night she called me again to share the excitement of the day. The wonderful atmosphere of God's power at work in peoples' lives so permeated the telephone wires that I felt almost like I had spent the day with her. Sunday morning the phone rang again, and in her concern for my well-being, she had taken time out from her busy schedule, just to remind me that she loved me. My eyes were going back to Christ, and each one of these calls helped. Then Sunday afternoon when I certainly didn't expect a call, she spent more money and time to talk to me again. You see, she was so considerate, when I really needed her, to spend a small amount of time and money to be as close to me as possible.

If women would only realize that even though we are said to be the strong ones in the family, we need, want and thrive on consideration from the "weaker" one in our family.

Since I find it better because of my nature to go to work early, often I come home exhausted and really too tired to be the pleasant person I like to be with Frances and Joanie. Frances quickly learned that if I slip off my shoes and socks and lie down flat on my back with my arms stretched along my sides, I can go to sleep for about twenty minutes and wake up completely refreshed and stay that way throughout the evening. She always has dinner ready when I come home from work, and when she sees me tired (and because she is considerate of the way I feel, she is observant about this) she takes me by the hand, leads me to the bedroom, removes my shoes and socks, or while I am taking them off she removes the bedspread, and within moments she has me tucked into bed, kisses me, turns off the lights, closes the blackout drapes and slips out of the room for the twenty minutes' rest I need. At the end of the twenty minutes I can depend on her to appear at my bedside and awaken me with kisses.

Now let's see another way she could handle this. She could immediately give me some annoying task to do, or start telling me about the things she has planned for the evening. But because she is considerate of my every need and desire, she doesn't have a single thing for me to do *until* I have had the little rest which is so vital for me. She could let me go and lie down by myself, but what man doesn't feel loved and wanted when his wife fluffs up the pillow for him, takes off his shoes, and tenderly kisses him as he lies down. While most men have a very independent nature, do you girls realize how very much we love to be catered to?

No man likes to come home to an empty house. When on rare occasions I arrive home and Frances is not there to greet me, I always have a sinking feeling. Once in a great while she has tried to phone me and I am not available, and she needs to slip away to the store. I always phone her when I leave the office, but if I don't catch her by phone, I can always depend on finding a note telling me where she is, letting me know she tried to reach me, and then adding some little love note. I appreciate how very considerate she is to try always to do her shopping early enough to be home to welcome me. Sounds like a little thing, doesn't it? But then you'll notice all the things that make a marriage happy are the *little* things.

I am sure that all the wives wash their husbands' clothes, but do you do the little extra things that let your husband know you're thinking about him? I was so surprised after Frances and I were first married to discover that she folds shorts and undershirts together, so that all I have to do is to pick up one neat package and to know that both are together. Now anyone knows it isn't hard to pick up two garments to put on, but I think it's just an extra expression of love and consideration to do this special little thing. There are many little things in this area, like matching socks, and putting different colors in different piles. Just a tiny little thing, but it shows consideration.

I'm a happy splasher when I shave and the basin is always a wet mess when I finish. I then take the dry wash cloth and quickly dry the chrome fixtures and the counter around the basin. This all takes maybe fifteen seconds. If it is left wet, spots set and are much harder to get off.

If I had to start my daily work with a dirty looking area, it would not exactly put a smile on my attitude. So, I want Frances to enjoy her first encounter of what's left of me after I go to work.

What do you girls do to keep interested in your husband's business? After all, this is what earns a living for your family. Are you considerate enough to even learn the names of his associates, his associates' wives, etc.? It surprised me how quickly Frances learned the names of all of my partners and their wives. As we shared the events of our day's activities she didn't just show her interest, she actually was interested in knowing all about what happened in my life.

Frances always tries to arrange her work and activities so we can spend all the time I have away from work together, doing the things we enjoy together. I find her the most exciting person in the world. I think if every couple would see how many little considerations they could give to each other and try hard to find things to do together, they would all discover that their mates are the most exciting people in their lives. The priceless pearl of marriage would be the most priceless possession in their lives. I'm with Frances every chance I get because I want to enjoy my treasure.

I have had many opportunities to observe the personal lives of couples and I see some with loving, exciting lives and some who are arguing and bickering and making sharp, cutting remarks to each other. One thing I always see in these couples is that the ones who have the exciting, loving, enjoyable lives show constant consideration for each other, and the ones who do not get along are rarely considerate of each other. There just is no doubt in my mind that any Christian couple can have an exciting marriage if they really want to. Being considerate is one of the most important demonstrations of love.

Just for fun, why don't you sit down right now and make a list of areas where you can be more considerate of your spouse. You never know what might happen as a result!

Be Fun to Live With

by Frances

If you had to choose one person to live with the rest of your life, would you choose you? Are you fun to live with, or does your disposition suffer at times? Would you honestly pick yourself to live with?

"Love . . . rejoices in the right" (1 Corinthians 13:6).

This Scripture has been and can be taken to mean many different things, but right now I've decided to use it in conjunction with the joy of marriage. Love "rejoices in the right." And isn't it right to want your marriage to be happy, and isn't it right to be fun to live with?

Did you ever participate in a BIG wedding? You know the planning, preparation, endless fittings of dresses, talks with the florist, talks with the minister, talks with the caterer, just talk, talk, talk with everybody. Then all of a sudden the big day arrives. You go in the church and sit down and before you know it, the bride is fluttering down the aisle, and before you can hardly get comfortable she's fluttering back down the aisle, and it's over. I wonder how many of us have been to weddings and made the statement, "It seemed so short—before I knew it, it was over!" And did it ever dawn on you what an incorrect statement this is? It isn't over at all, it's just beginning. They have the job of living with each other for the next forty or fifty years, and when I say "job" I mean just that, because to be married and to be fun to live with is a regular job and you have to go to work every day to be successful.

Charles and I celebrated our first Christmas as husband and wife in a most unusual way. Our daughter Joan was spending the holidays in Miami. So Charles and I decided, instead of cooking at home for just the two of us we would go out to a nice restaurant and have an exciting time just talking to each other. We would enjoy all the things which go with a festive Christmas dinner without having to go to the trouble of cooking them, and cleaning up afterwards. Mid-afternoon we went out and got in the car and made a very interesting discovery! Charles discovered that when he came home the day before, he had forgotten and left the parking lights on. As a result, the battery was run down, so the car wouldn't start. This wasn't a problem because we have a second car. Even though Joan, who drives it to school daily, said it needed some work done on it, we knew it was in running condition.

We decided because of the possibility of trouble in the second car, we would push the first car out into the street, then with the second car we would get it started, and by running it a little, the battery would be back up high enough for us to drive wherever we were going. It really sounded so simple, but it wasn't! After we had backed my car out,

75

Charles got in his, I got in mine to push him, and neither of them would start. I tried and tried to start mine, and then Charles came back to see if he could start it. About thirty to forty-five minutes later we were still standing in the middle of our street with two cars which weren't working.

Did you ever try to get a garage on Christmas day? They just aren't open, and I don't blame them, so we didn't even try. Did we get mad? We did not. We looked at each other and said, "Praise the Lord, anyway." We pushed the cars as best we could back to the curb, turned and walked up the driveway to the house singing, "I Am So Glad That Jesus Loves Me."

I went into the kitchen to see what I could find in the refrigerator to cook for Christmas dinner. While it might not have been the usual Christmas type of dinner, we loved it.

Charles said many wives would have yelled at their husbands about being dumb and leaving the lights on, but somehow or other I thought the situation was hilarious. Here we sat, with two cars, and neither car in running condition. Think of the tension that could have been created in a situation like this. Think of how frustrated both of us could have been. Think how easy it might have been to say things that could have spoiled our first Christmas together, but both Charles and I think the other is fun to live with and so our first Christmas was fabulous, even though it was a little unique. Being fun to live with can certainly cut down on the temper explosions in any home. And what good do they do, anyway?

Charles is not mechanically inclined, to say the least. But then I don't know of anyone who is perfect in *everything*, do you? If I wanted the best C.P.A. in the world, I'd call on my husband. But if something is mechanically wrong, I would call for someone else.

One Saturday I had decided to clean the oven and since I'm talking about people not being mechanically inclined, I should mention myself first. My intentions are always so good, but my ability isn't so good. I got so far, then I got stuck and couldn't get one of the racks out. Charles decided to help me, even though he had warned me not to do the job, but to let someone who knew how to work on it. Well, we pulled and shoved, and pulled and shoved, and pushed and heaved, and finally by the sheer strength of the two of us, we removed the troublesome part. We managed to get the stove cleaned, and then when we decided to put things back together again, it just didn't fit.

Charles could have really yelled at me about that time, because I had about asphyxiated us with the oven cleaner I was using. He had told me not to do it in the first place. We kept looking at each other and saying, "Praise the Lord, anyway." I still don't know of anything better in a crisis situation than those four words. We finally got the oven back together again, not by our own cleverness, but by sheer willpower and prayer (mostly prayer). Charles and I both decided we are not mechanically inclined, so we're going to leave that kind of work to other people.

Maybe the reason we made that grand statement

was one of the things that happened right after we were married. When I moved to Houston and into our house, after a month or so, I decided in my good housewifely way that we ought to take the wax off the kitchen floor because it was much too thick. I told Charles that I thought I'd do this, and he insisted that he didn't want me doing such hard work. I thought he was trying to protect me since I was a bride, so I decided to go ahead and take up the wax. Anyone who has ever removed thick, old wax from a kitchen floor (especially when it's about six inches thick) knows what a horrible job this is. Houston is warm most of the time and it wasn't only warm this day, it was HOT.

I had bought some of this miracle stuff that you just put on the floor, let it sit for three minutes, and then "whisk it away" with one little swipe of a damp cloth. I let it sit for three minutes. Nothing happened! Then I let it sit for ten minutes. Nothing happened! Then I let it sit for thirty minutes. Nothing happened! I finally got down on my hands and knees with a hard scrub brush to try and loosen the wax with this wonderful miracle wax remover, and after about two hours of intensive scrubbing, my back was broken, my hands felt like they were about to fall off, and the floor was one big sticky, gooey mess.

By this time I felt like crying because I knew Charles was going to be home soon and the kitchen was the saddest mess I have ever seen anywhere. I rinsed the same little spot about twenty times, and it was still gooey. About that time, Charles drove up and I ran out to meet him, all sweaty and smelly instead of my usual way. He took one look at me and said, "You've been trying to take the wax off the floor, haven't you?"

What could I say? I had to admit it because there wasn't any hiding what I was doing. Even though he kissed me tenderly, I'm sure he wanted to shake me real hard for not doing as he had asked me to. Then he decided the only thing to do was to get a commercial company to come in and do it. But the next day our maid came to clean the house, and she and I decided after putting our heads together that if I rented an electric waxer with a steel pad on it, we would get the wax off the floor. So out I sailed to get the electric waxer, thinking how proud Charles would be of me, because when I called a commercial company, they wanted over fifty dollars to do a floor the size of my kitchen floor, and I thought that was ridiculous.

I rented the biggest floor waxer they had because I knew this would do the job quickly, lugged it out to the car, drove home, lugged it out of the car, and started to work. I turned the electricity on and before I knew what was happening, the waxer had dragged me all the way across the kitchen, and banged into the kitchen cabinet, making a nice dent mark. I quickly turned it off and felt like I had a tiger on my hands. By this time my daughter had gotten home from school. We decided we would both hold the waxer and then turn the switch on. We did . . . and it almost knocked both of us upside down, and again it ran into the cabinet. Not only did it run into the cabinet (as the machine was having a wild, mad time making un-understandable circles all over the place), it also slopped this miracle wax remover and particles of the soft wax all over the cabinets. (We're still trying to get it off.)

We decided after this that the big waxer just wasn't for us, so we cleaned the brushes, and then lugged it out to the car, took it to the store and rented a much smaller one. We got home with the smaller one, confident that this would really do it! Then we started. We could control the smaller one, but it wasn't powerful enough to do anything. So we ran out to the garage and brought in all the hard scrub brushes we could find. Miss Molly, our beloved maid, Joan and I all got down on our hands and knees and tried to literally pick the wax off with our fingernails. We scrubbed, we scraped, we groaned, we strained, we prayed, we rinsed, we struggled until I felt the entire world was a big glob of gummy wax. We used steel wool, we used paint scrapers, we used everything all of us could think of. Good old Miss Molly, she's such a wonderful Christian. I'm sure if she hadn't been she would have quit that day right on the spot. But we all kept struggling, trying to get the floor done.

After a day of this, I was so stiff I could hardly move, and we had to leave early the next morning on a weekend trip to a church, and I still couldn't move. My poor body ached the entire weekend.

Well, we came home after the weekend, and the floor had begun to show some signs of a few places being back to the natural floor, but it was still a very unglorious mess. As Charles started to work in the morning he said in that very sweet, but very stern way he has, "Don't you touch that floor until I get home. Promise?" I wasn't about to try to do anything with it because my muscles were really sore by this time, so I promised not to touch the floor. And I didn't! In the first place, he didn't have to worry about my doing anything because I was so stiff and sore from the unaccustomed hard physical work, that I could hardly bend over to get my shoes on. My shoulders ached, my arms ached, my legs ached, my back ached and I was generally a mess.

When Charles came home that night, we quickly ate supper, then he put on his work clothes and started on the floor. His hands are so strong he could accomplish a lot more than I ever did. Even so, it took almost four hours for him to get the floor in presentable shape. All this time, I was concerned that he would have a heart attack and I prayed and prayed and prayed as he worked and sweated and worked and sweated. Finally it was all done. But before it was, I had mentally been counting the cost: 15 or so cans of miracle wax remover at $3.00 per can; 4 large boxes of powdered "aid to removing wax" at 97¢ per box; rental of large and small waxing machines, $3.50; purchase of steel wool pad for machine, 98¢, 2 scrubbing brushes with hard bristles, $4.00; gas for three trips to the store, $2.00; and this is not counting Miss Molly's labor, Joan's labor, my labor, and most of all, Charles' labor.

When Charles had finished the floor, he emptied the buckets, went in and showered, came out and put his arms around me very firmly (but oh so sweetly) and said, "Honey, will you promise me never to do anything like that again?" I'll give you three guesses what I said.

Now, can you imagine what many husbands would have done had they been in Charles' shoes? I am sure that many marriages have been wrecked by less than this. But Charles recognized my motives in trying to do the job myself. He was aware of the fact that I was trying to save money, even though in the long run it cost us far more than if we had had it done commercially. He didn't yell and scream at me. Because he's fun to live with, he made the most of a situation I had gotten myself involved in and he pulled us out of it without even a ripple on the surface or underneath the surface of our marriage. I shudder when I think of what some husbands might have done under the same circumstances. Have you ever gotten yourself into the same interesting situation with these do-it-yourself jobs around the house?

When Charles and I first began traveling together, we became aware of some of the hardships that exist when you travel around. Now please don't misunderstand me, I don't really consider them to be hardships, but let's just say they're experiences.

Charles and I have slept in many places all over the United States during our honeymoon year—some ultra elegant, and some, well—some not so ultra elegant. Some were ultra private and some, well—some not so ultra private. But do you know, we've had the most beautiful fellowship in the world with people whose homes have not been ultra elegant.

I am thinking in particular of one home where we stayed. When we got there at night, we had had a tremendous day consisting of flying, waiting in airports, and then riding 200 miles in a car. The weather was cold and we had had to get up so early in the morning that we were both completely exhausted, when we finally did get to our destination.

After the first service we were taken to where we were to stay, and we started to go to bed. I got into my nightgown first and as I sat down on the edge of the bed, the bed collapsed. I said, "Charles, you'd better do something about this bed." So, God love Charles, he put the slats back in and I sat down again on the edge of the bed, only this time I sat very gently, and would you believe it, the *bed fell down again.*

I said to Charles, "Honey, maybe I weigh too much for this bed. Why don't you lie down on it the next time you fix it and see what happens." So Charles fixed it again. He got the slats and put them back in again. He sat down . . . and *the bed fell down again.* We decided that maybe if we got in a horizontal position and sort of rolled ourselves into the bed it might work. So we rolled ourselves into the bed, but *the bed fell down again!* Poor Charles, he was so exhausted because we had had such a hectic day too.

Are you aware what could have happened to his disposition? Many times we vent our anger on our mate when it isn't anybody's fault, but I thank God that both Charles and I think about each other instead of ourselves. I suggested, "Honey, why don't we just sleep on the bed as it is, and not be concerned about the fact that it's collapsed," and so that's exactly what we did. We just slept with me hanging onto one side of the bed, and Charles hanging onto me to keep him from rolling onto the floor.

It was quite an unusual night. We could have become very annoyed with the situation. We might even have been irritated that we didn't have better accommodations than this. Because Charles and I really want to be fun to live with, we just had a good laugh and giggled so loud and hard that it's a miracle we didn't wake everybody up. This can really do an awful lot for your marriage. Instead of one getting mad and putting the other one completely on edge, if both people are relaxed and fun to live with it's amazing how much more enjoyable it can make your entire marriage.

The thing we're trying to point out in this story is that if a husband and wife stand together in any situation, it can be fun, it can be enjoyable, it can be exciting, it can be a good experience. How many times, though, couples do not stand together. It's *me* against *you*, or *you* against *me!* This is one of the saddest things in the world when couples forget that they are *one*, and not two.

Probably some time in your life while you have been on a vacation, you've stopped at a motel or hotel, trailer cabin, or camped out where the accommodations were not nearly as good as you would have liked for them to have been. Just think back right now, what was your reaction at that moment? Was it really good, or was it really bad? Did you take it out on your mate because something went wrong that you didn't like, or did you both just relax and enjoy it together because you're fun to live with?

Well, we like the way we do it. We like the way that God has dealt in both of our lives because we both believe that love rejoices with the right. We believe that our marriage is right, and are going to keep right on loving it, in spite of all the little circumstances which plague every marriage.

Did you ever make a wrong purchase and then have to live with it? Well, I did. One of the things I have always liked to do is to sleep on a hard bed. A soft bed can really ruin my rest. When Charles and I were married, we decided to purchase a new mattress and springs for our bed. I asked him what kind he liked. He said whatever I liked was fine with him. I insisted that I loved a hard mattress, the harder the better. He said if that was what would make me happy, we would get one, even though he thought possibly a medium hard one would be better. And so we did! We bought the hardest mattress that's made. I excitedly waited for the mattress to get here because even though it had felt a little hard to me in the store, I knew that we would get used to it and then we'd really love it.

Well, the great day came, and the mattress arrived. As soon as it was set up in the bedroom, Joan decided to bounce on it, so she plunked herself down on it, expecting to have a nice bounce for herself. She went thud! She looked at me most peculiarly and said, "Don't you think this is a little hard? It feels worse than the floor." I gaily replied, "No, I don't think it's too hard, because you know I *like* hard mattresses." She picked herself up, turned around and tried to test the mattress with her hand, and it didn't give even a fraction of an inch. I sat down on it and secretly thought it was the hardest mattress I had ever seen.

Charles called to find out if the new mattress had been delivered and I said, "Yes." He asked, "Is it hard enough for you?" I cringed when he said that but I replied, "Yes, it's hard enough," wondering how in the world we could sleep on something that hard. Then he said, "Do you like it, honey?" I said, "The mattress cover is pretty. The mattress is a little hard, but we'll get used to it." Well, Charles came home and we couldn't wait to try out the new bed. He managed to get his pajamas on first, and plopped down on the bed! You should have seen the shocked look on his face!—like he had thrown himself down on a rock pile!

I don't know when we went to bed that night, but I do know we didn't stay there all night. After about forty-five minutes or so, I said to Charles, "Honey, does this make your shoulders hurt?" He said, "Yes, it does; as a matter of fact I think I'll get out of bed for a little while and massage my shoulder." Next it was my turn to get out of bed because by that time my hip felt like it had been paralyzed. Charles helped me out of bed and we walked around a little and then went back to bed again. This kept up all night long and when morning came we decided that neither of us had slept very well, but since it was the first night, we knew the next one would be better. But it wasn't.

Of course bedding isn't returnable after you have slept on it, so we had no choice except to learn to sleep in it, and so we did. We have laughed more during the "breaking in" period of the bed because of the sore shoulders we've had, but we have learned a lot, too. We could have complained about the bed—Charles could have yelled at me because I'm the one who wanted the hard bed, or we could have looked on it as a situation to draw us closer together, and that's what we did.

I insist to Charles that I was a real nut for buying such a hard mattress, and because of my being willing to take the blame, Charles has always run to my rescue and says, "It's not so hard, honey, it just takes time to get used to a mattress." So together we have learned to be fun to live with even when you're sleeping on a rock slab.

We laugh a lot—never at each other, but in joy, *together*. Charles says I'm fun to live with because I can laugh at myself, and I can admit that I'm wrong, and praise the Lord, I can say the same thing about him. A sense of humor and the ability for each of us to see ourselves as we really are can help a lot of problems in marriage. Why don't you and your husband each make a little list of the things you think make your mate fun to live with? How about making a list about yourself and see how many of your characteristics make you fun to live with?

Be Desirous

by Frances

As I wrote the name of this chapter, many thoughts came into my mind. There are so many ways this chapter could be written—about how to be desirous to your mate, which things to be desirous of in life, which line of desires to pursue. But this chapter is really not about that at all. Good old Webster defines the word "desire" as, "to wish earnestly for, crave; to express a wish for" or as a noun, "a longing for the possession of some object; an earnest wish, a request, the object longed for."

I like Psalm 37:4 which says, "Take delight in the Lord, and He will give you the desires of your heart." In other words, He will give you the thing you wish earnestly for. Probably the most important thing in marriage except Christ is the desire to make your marriage beautiful, or to make it work as many people say. Isn't it fabulous to know that God is helping your marriage succeed because He wants to give you the desires of your heart.

Think about the word "desire" in many other areas of life. If you're going to have company for dinner, you "wish earnestly" that the dinner will come out just right, so you put all your attention, knowledge and skill into making the dinner perfect. You don't let anything come between you and the dinner. The same thing is true of an artist who paints a picture. He puts everything he's got into the painting. If he sincerely does this, his painting will reveal it. If he's just slipshod, the painting will reflect poor quality. Have you ever watched a skilled dressmaker sew? The dressmaker doesn't compromise with a shoddy seam or a part that's not cut right—she works on it until it is perfect. Did you ever see a skilled carpenter make a cabinet—sanding down, measuring, matching, until everything is perfect? Can you imagine the kind of carpentry work Jesus did? Would it have been half-hearted and sloppy? Of course not.

Exactly the same thing happens in marriage. If the desire of our heart is for our marriage to be as perfect as two humans can make it, it will be, because we will put all of our attention, knowledge and skill into making it perfect. Marriage is like everything else—you can't do it halfway and expect it to be all the way. You can't cook your dinner on the stove if you don't turn the stove on. I could prepare the most scrumptious stew in the world, but if I didn't turn on the burner of my stove, I doubt if the stew would be palatable. So it is in marriage—we must be willing to go all the way. If you don't want your marriage to work, it won't. You might be able to endure each other, but who wants just to endure, when God promises so much in marriage.

When God gave me Charles to be my husband, I wanted more than anything in the world to have our marriage perfect. I had a desire to attain the happiness in marriage that God Himself ordained. So I went into marriage with the idea of doing everything that was necessary to secure the desired results. As you read this book you will discover lots of places where I had to change my ways to keep my marriage from getting problem ridden. The desire has always been out in front with never a thought concerning what I might be giving up. And really, isn't it the same way with Christ? Before we become Christians we think of a lot of the things we have to give up. Then we discover that Christ gives so much more in return that we really haven't given up a single thing. And the same thing is true in marriage. Marriage in its true sense gives so much more to the people involved than they would ever have to give up.

If you read my preceding book *My Love Affair with Charles,* you know that God only gave us eleven days' advance notice as to when we were going to be married, and this was only three days before Charles was scheduled to leave Houston to come to Miami. The house that was to be my home was still the same as when Charles' wife had died. All the family pictures were still around. Many personal items were still there because of a lack of time or reason for removing them. Because Charles had exactly the same desire as I had, he managed to have two wonderful Christian women come over to the house and go through the entire house and remove anything in the house which might have reminded me that another woman had been Charles's wife.

I don't know how they ever did it, but they did! And when Charles brought me into our home for the first time there was nothing to indicate that any-one else had ever lived there. Charles recognized the fact that we can't look back, and thereby solved one of the greatest problems which exist in second marriages today. Jeanne *was* his wife: I *am* his wife.

So many times, especially with young people, they want to hang on to their past. He still wants to go out with the boys, she still wants to see her girl friends occasionally. Nothing in the world hurts a marriage as much as the desire to retain part of our past life in our present life. I have never known a marriage that worked successfully where either one held on to the past.

We were counseling with a young couple recent-ly who had separated and she was on her way home to mama because he was still spending nights out with the boys. She couldn't understand this, so she complained. He rebelled, got sarcastic and mean, and before they knew it, they were at swords points.

The Bible says, "For this cause a man shall leave his father and mother, and shall cleave to his wife; and the two shall become one flesh" (Eph. 5:31). And it means not only mother and father, but friends as well.

What does a married man have in common with a single man? Not much if you're honest. And what does a married woman have in common with a sin-gle woman? Not much. The single people will make the married people envious because of their free-dom—the fact that each has his own money to spend, etc. So if old friends are to continue, it *must* be on a joint basis, and not just for the husband to continue with his old friends, or the wife to continue with her old friends.

Many marriages are miserable today because men like to hunt and fish, and as a result leave their wives at home to be "deer" widows or "bait" for some unsuspecting sin to come into their lives. Unfortunately ego comes back into our life when our mate chooses to do something else other than be with us, so we decide we have to do something, too! And this is where trouble begins. I wonder how come Adam left Eve alone long enough for her to be tempted by the serpent? I have heard men say, "They just want to get away from everything for a while," so they go hunting or fishing so they can relax. I pray that my husband never has the desire to get away from me. And if I were a woman whose husband wanted to go fishing and deer hunting to relax I would look at my own life and determine what caused me not to be the relaxing agent he needed in his life.

So it all comes back to the same old "desire"—do you want to be a good deer hunter, or do you want to be an excellent husband. If two people are truly one, then their desires must be the same. They should search out a mutual fun thing, maybe even deer hunting, *together!* You'll think I'm being idealistic, but I'm not! Take a good look at the marriages you know and see if I'm not right.

Another young couple we counseled with recently had gone their separate ways because he wanted his freedom. I asked him what he meant by "freedom." He said, "Freedom to do what I want to do, to come and go as I please, and not have to report to anyone." What he was really saying was, "I want to continue in sin, and I don't want anyone to interfere with my pleasure in sin." Actually, he had no desire to make the marriage a success, because if he had, the desire for pleasure outside of marriage would have been gone.

Charles and I have all the freedom we want. We can come and go as we please, and we don't have to report to anyone. The reason—we're free to live in Christ, therefore we have no desire to be other than what God wants us to be. We have forsaken all others, and cling to each other. We have no desire to go anywhere, even to the store, unless we are together because we believe that God Himself made us one. We can come and go as we please, because each of us pleases to please the other. We don't have to report to each other, but we naturally want to share everything that's happened during the day when we have been separated. I think my husband is the most interesting man in the world, and I would rather listen to him than anyone else I know of. So I'm going to spend my time with him, and the better I get to know him, the better I like him, so I'm going to continue getting to know him better.

by Charles

Frances mentioned to me the other day that she thought it was interesting that all the newspaper and magazine ads pertaining to being desirous, lovable, seductive, charming, glamorous and interesting were all addressed to women, and she wanted to know why they were never addressed to the men. She wanted to know if the world doesn't think it's necessary for men to be alluring and desirous, too. The more I thought about this, the more I realized the emphasis is put on the woman to be the desirous one. And then many men wonder why certain things come up in marriage.

If a woman has to do all the alluring, charming and glamorizing something is wrong with the marriage! Why should a woman do all the attracting? The more you give in marriage, the more you get in return, so men, you ought to think about making yourselves more desirous.

There are so many tiny little areas where we fall down. Is your deodorant always doing full duty? How about your breath? Are you clean shaven? Do you try to look sharp and fresh? Is your hair trimmed? Do you keep a bright shine on your shoes? Do you walk in a slouch, or do you walk with a bounce? Do you keep a happy expression on your face and excitement in your conversation with your wife and family? Do you have a positive, joyful attitude?

It is amazing how many men expect their wives to have all the glamorous characteristics of the dating days, and yet they don't think they have to do a thing in return. One of the best principles in marriage that I know of is, "It is better to give than to receive." When we are thinking about how we can please our mates, and how we can be desirable to our mates, then we're not thinking selfishly about ourselves and have turned our desires outward instead of inward.

Exactly the same principle applies where Christ is concerned. If we give Him our lives, He gives us back so much more in return. When we give all of ourselves to our wives, they give back so much more in return. If your marriage isn't operating at that level right now, I'd suggest you sit down and take a look to see where the trouble started, when it started, and who started it; and then start being honest with each other and both of you think about being more desirable, lovable, charming and interesting. I still don't think all those adjectives apply to women only. If we men worked as hard at marriage as our wives do, there wouldn't be so many failures. If a new secretary came along in your office, and things weren't going so well at home, the first thing you might be tempted to do is try and make yourself "desirous" to her. Just remember, practicing being desirous at home pays a far greater dividend.

Frances and I visited in a home recently where the husband was so grumpy we wanted to leave the minute we got there. I wondered how desirable he thought he was. Many times, as the breadwinner in the family, we think we don't have to try and be desirable, because we've got the woman right where we want her—dependent upon us. But why live on garbage when you can have steak? How much happier is your marriage going to be when your wife knows you're supporting her because you love her, and not because you have to because she's your wife?

I look at homes, too, where the woman does all the disciplining of the children, and the man just sits there like a bump on a log. How desirable are you, not only as a husband, but as a father when you let your wife do all the disciplining? How desirable are you for your children to look up to when they don't see you behaving as a father should? How desirable are you in their eyes when they see you treat their mother as a servant? How much love does your family feel in you? Children are pretty smart, and they learn fast.

Turn your *desires* toward making your marriage an exciting one and see what happens in front of your very own eyes. Keep your thinking like this, "The desire of my heart is to make my marriage exciting." Say this every day if yours isn't that way right now, and it won't be long before it will really be exciting!

Be Forgiving

by Frances

"If you are angry, don't sin by nursing your grudge. Don't let the sun go down with you still angry—get over it quickly; for when you are angry you give a mighty foothold to the devil" (Ephesians 4:26-27).

True, true, true! Of course it is. Let's all learn to use the words, "I'm sorry," often in our marriage. Those two little words are magic words, and yet they are often the hardest words in the English language to say, especially to the one we love.

Have you ever burned your husband's toast on the morning when he was late getting out of the house, and there wasn't time to put in another piece? As you scraped it off, were you careful to say, "I'm sorry, honey, that isn't a very good way to send you to work, is it?" And he might say back, "That's O.K., honey. Don't worry about it—I'll eat an early lunch."

Can you imagine all kinds of other ways this situation could have turned out? He could have yelled, "You know I don't like burned toast," and gone out the door, slamming it behind him, saying, "Well, I can get a decent piece of toast at the coffee shop," and then harbored a grudge all day.

Of course, I'd suggest the wife get up in time to

fix the toast properly, and if she burns it, she can make another piece. But just supposing the situation happened this way, see how any future trouble could have been avoided by her saying, "I'm sorry," and his attitude being one of forgiveness.

Think of how much God had to forgive us when we became Christians—WOW! Maybe He didn't have to forgive very much in your life. In mine He had a great big old slate to wipe off, but He did it, without a single complaint on His part, but with just tremendous love, love, love, and He let me know that He loved me. I'm sure if I had said to Him the day after I became a Christian, "God, how in the world did You ever manage to forgive all that sin at one time?" God would have answered, "What sin?" You see, He had forgiven me and had buried it in the deepest sea, never to be thought of again. And since we are made in the image of God, let us practice behaving like we were made in that image. Let's start forgiving these little things before they grow into big things and bury them in the deepest sea, never to be thought of again.

I'll have to share a funny story with you, even though it really isn't funny. Recently a couple were divorced because he said, "She deliberately burned my toast every morning." You can imagine how this started off with a piece of toast accidentally burned, and then one thing led to another. This might sound ridiculous, but are you aware of the fact that most divorces started off because of a ridiculous situation a long time before the marriage reached the exploding point?

I was privileged to do some counseling recently

with a couple who had been to see a divorce lawyer because they were completely incompatible. They couldn't communicate with each other. They could hardly stand each other's company. Each criticized everything about the other. They knew that divorce was the only way out, and yet they both were Christians. Now how do we solve a situation like this? Neither Charles nor I are psychologists, but we do know that the love of God can overcome any and all situations, and we always try to steer clear of the problems, and point the people to Christ. Instead of pointing to the problem, point to the solution and completely take your eyes off of the problem. This can immediately make you forgiving, believe it or not!

The wife in this case was unusually attractive—the husband more or less ordinary. She had the kind of figure all the men would turn around and look at. He had a sour look which might make you tend to run from him. I had been invited to their home for dinner and when we sat down to dinner, it was beautiful—roast pork, applesauce, mashed potatoes, gravy, peas and the usual things that go with that kind of a dinner, including hot rolls and butter, and blueberry pie with coffee.

After the husband said the blessing, the conversation went something like this:

"How come we're having roast pork tonight? You said we were going to have turkey."

She said, "Well, the store had nice pork roasts today and so many times they're not available, and I know how you like pork, so I thought you might like this for a change."

He insisted, "Well, you said turkey, and since you said turkey, you should have had turkey."

Now let me ask you, what difference did it really make?

And then he said, "You know I like french fries, why did we have to have mashed potatoes?"

And she replied, "Well, honey, pork makes such good gravy, I thought you'd like to have that for a change."

Then we got to the hot rolls and he wanted to know why she had put them in the bun warmer when they really were so much better if she warmed them in the oven. When we got to blueberry pie, he wanted to know why she hadn't baked cherry pie. All of this was completely inconsequential, wasn't it?

Were any of his complaints justified? As long as roast pork was one of his favorites, did it make any difference if she had cooked this? And since he liked both mashed potatoes and french fries, why make such a federal case out of how the potatoes were cooked? And as for the pie, what difference did it make if it was cherry or blueberry. I almost got indigestion as I ate my food because I wondered how in the world they had stayed together if that's the way all their mealtimes were eaten. I would have developed an ulcer long ago, I decided.

And then I watched a very interesting situation. They had three children, all under five. The great critic who apparently felt like he was doing them a favor to come home and eat, did nothing to help with the children. Did you ever sit at a table with three little children under five? It's an experience to say the least! And all he did was to yell at her to keep the kids quiet and to get them fed quickly. Did you ever try to cut meat for three kids at one time? Did you ever try to keep two kids in high chairs happy while you were fixing plates for three? And did you ever have guests in the middle of all this? Try it sometime and see what happens.

THEN . . . he complained about the way the roast was cooked. He said it wasn't done enough. She replied that since he always complained because she burned everything, she had gotten to the point where she was afraid to cook anything long enough for fear it would be too done or would be burned!

I decided to inject a little love into the evening meal, so I ventured the idea, "How many times did you kiss her when you came home tonight?" He looked at me as if I had flipped my wig or something but didn't answer. I kept quiet during the rest of the dinner. It was noisy enough with the two of them yelling at each other politely and cuttingly, and I really prayed that God would give me an opportunity to talk to each one of them separately.

And God did just that. He let me talk to the woman first. She shared with me the fact that her husband went out every night to some sort of a church function or Boy Scouts or something of that nature. This left her with the responsibility of putting the children to bed, getting the house straightened up, getting the dishes done, and then collapsing by the time he came home, and being completely frustrated and ready to chop his head off at the first word he said. I asked her why he took on these responsibilities for every night of the week, and asked her if she ever went along. She said that occasionally she did, but she would have to always watch all the children and for this reason it was easier to stay home.

I asked her what it was about her that irritated him. I asked her if she met him with love and kisses at the door and she said, "He's just not the affectionate type." She had tried this a couple of times and it didn't work, so she wasn't going to do it anymore, and now they just never bothered kissing each other. I suggested that she have everything in good shape when he came home the next night and greet him at the door with a real loving kiss.

She also liked to work in the business world and had taken a part-time job, working five hours a day. He had been wanting her to give this up, but she liked the freedom the job gave her, and she wasn't about to give it up. I asked her what her relationship to God was, and had she asked God about the job and whether or not she should give it up. So many times we take the ordinary run of the day's problems out of God's hands and try to solve them ourselves, without realizing that God can solve them much better than we can. We had a good long talk into the wee hours of the morning and she decided that she had let the problems of the world come between her and her relationship to God. So I encouraged her to begin praying about even the most minute little situations, asking God to give her direction in all areas.

Then, believe it or not, God provided the opportunity for me to talk to the husband alone. In talking to him, I discovered that he wasn't the affectionate type. His family had never been, and it just wasn't his nature to be affectionate. I asked him how often he told his wife he loved her, and he replied, "She knows I love her." I replied, "That's great, but how often do you tell her this fact?" He hemmed and hawed and said, "Well, I bring home my paycheck, and she can use the car whenever she wants, and she has everything she needs. Isn't that enough?" I said, "Nope, it's not enough. Every woman likes to be told she's loved."

Then I asked him if he honestly wanted his marriage to be successful. I asked him if he thought being married to anyone else would be any better and if he wanted to turn his three little children loose to be raised by a mother who might get married again to someone who could be a miserable father. As he saw what the future might possibly hold, he cried out, "Help me, help me!" We prayed and asked God to break his stony, critical heart, and to give him instead a soft, loving, tender heart, and God did just that!

Here were two people who sincerely loved each other, and yet whose marriage was on the rocks because they were not looking to God as the source of power in their marriage. Yet both of them had a sincere desire to be Christian all the way, but each was letting *ego* come in between them. Both of them gave themselves in total surrender to God, and it has been exciting to see them at various intervals and share what has happened in their lives. I would like to quote just a few lines from a recent letter from her.

"Oh, how God knows what's best for us—and we're just too blind to see this most of the time. When you stayed with us I prayed that God would do whatever He could to make me spiritually what I should be. And little did I realize how He would do it. Frances, I can't tell you how much I appreciate you and Charles for listening to God when He sent you here. He knew I needed you and your example of total surrender to Him. How very PERFECT is His plan for us when we let Him have His way!

"My husband is a new person, too. Although he was a little more of a stubborn personality to work with, God in His divine way slowly and gently turned my husband into total surrender. Up until now he was afraid to let go for God. Thank God for His continued goodness to us! How very patient He is with us, and how undeserving we all are!"

Where did this miracle start? It started with each of them forgiving the other, just exactly the way our life with Christ starts, with God forgiving us for whatever we've done in the past, and wiping the slate clean. This couple forgave each other, wiped the slate clean, and started their marriage all over again. She forgave the previous coldness of his heart. He forgave her wanting to be a career girl. She forgave his criticism, he forgave her lack of love. In other words, they forgave and *forgot* all the things that had kept their marriage from being a success. And when I say ALL, I mean *everything*, because no couple can truly start afresh until everything in the past is wiped out in complete forgiveness, and buried in the deepest sea, never to be thought of again.

Their willingness to forgive each other came because of a surrender of their total lives to God and being willing to let God do what He wanted with their lives. Charles made a statement the other night which I thought was tremendous, so I'm going to share it with you. He said, "Salvation is the door through which every husband (groom) should carry his wife (bride) to enter a really exciting marriage." Think about that statement and see how easy that makes it to forgive the past in your marriage and start all over again.

Be Loyal

by Charles and Frances

I love the *Living New Testament's* seventh verse in 1 Corinthians 13. "If you love someone you will be loyal to him no matter what the cost. You will always believe in him, always expect the best of him, and always stand your ground in defending him."

Isn't that absolutely beautiful? The more I read about what God says about love, the more convinced I am the world certainly would not be in the shape it is in if we all got into the Word of God to hear what He has to say about the way we love our mates. "You will be loyal to him, no matter what the cost."

How many times has a man stepped out to open a new business, and the wife who is concerned with security said, "I told you you shouldn't have quit your job where you had security. You should have kept that regular paycheck instead of wasting all of our money going into business for yourself."

This could be the typical comment when a man has gone into business for himself, and temporarily it looks like things might not be going in the right direction. Above all other times, this is when a man needs a loyal wife. He needs to know that she loves him regardless of whether he is a success or failure in business. The world condemns us pretty quickly when things go wrong. And who is a man going to turn to when the going really gets rough and the world condemns him? Shouldn't his wife be right there loyal to him, believing in him, and standing her ground in defending him? So many times a woman bows to the pressures of those who talk about her husband and agrees with them concerning his behavior. I can't help but admire the woman who stands behind her husband all the way.

One of the greatest ways to show loyalty to your spouse is never to take your problems outside of your own home. Every couple should honestly promise on the day of their marriage never to include another person in their marriage—his mother, her mother, his sister, her sister, his best friend, her best friend, but forsaking all others, cleave only to each other. If at that moment when our love is so great we want only to belong to each other, we would promise with all the fervency of our hearts never to take a problem outside the walls of our marriage, and mean it, many problems could be avoided. When we take a problem outside of marriage, we are being disloyal because we are criticizing an act or attitude of our mate. If we are tempted to tell someone about our husband's faults, we should immediately remember the love we had for each other when we stood there promising before God to love each other until "death us do part." Even before that, do you remember those tender vows you gave to each other in secret with only God listening, promising to always be patient, tender and forgiving, even in areas of difficulty? The vows you made with just God listening are as binding and sacred as any other vows you might have made.

Do not tell your misunderstandings outside of the home because it only increases and exaggerates the trouble. It never settles it. There are many who will listen to your troubles and pretend to be your friends. But if you will talk to God about your situation you will find a much more loving, listening ear. You will find someone who will give you the true solutions to your problems and who will never turn His back on you. If we will remember that we are all human, and each of us has his faults and all of us will make mistakes somewhere along the line, then we can be tender, loving and willing to forgive and forget.

A husband looks to his wife for encouragement, for cheerfulness and confidence. No matter what the world may say or think—people may forget him, neglect him, lose confidence in him and turn their back on him, but a wife must not, because her love and loyalty to her husband may be the inspiration he needs to keep him going when the going gets rough.

A wife looks to her husband for protection in all things. Sometimes our bodies wear out physically even when we are still young. Sometimes we have a physical problem which changes our disposition and attitudes. This is a time when a wife needs her husband the most, needs his protection and loyalty to a greater degree than usual. This is when she needs his tenderness, kindness, patience and understanding. She doesn't need to hear him tell other people about how she cannot keep up with the housework or the children. A wife already knows this when she has been physically downed—and she needs encouragement until she is physically on top again.

Recently I went to the hospital to visit a woman who has cancer throughout her whole body. Her husband had brought her down here from another state. Instead of leaving her to go through the treatments by herself, he slept on a sofa in her room for her entire stay here (and not a very soft sofa at that). His loyalty to her was something that we felt the minute we entered the room. And the loyalty was not a forced thing, it was a beautiful thing. He was there because he loved her!

Love should always encourage loyalty. Loyalty should always mean loving "in spite of." It means loving and understanding when our mate gains an excessive amount of weight for no good reason, and seems unable to lose it. Loyalty means loving our husband when his hair gets thin or he gets bald. Loyalty means seeing the best in the one we love. Loyalty means devotion to the vows we made when we were married.

Under the heading of loyalty I would have to put something concerning the discipline of children in the family. While we all love our children, there are many times when discipline can really separate a man and his wife if they are not loyal to each other. In the dictionary the word loyalty is defined as "devotion to a cause." And in this case, the cause would be marriage.

Understanding children and how to raise them is a difficult task at best. When Charles (who had no children by his previous marriage) and I were married, he acquired my sixteen-year-old daughter. (She is now *ours* since he legally adopted her.) I left on a ten-day trip the day after she arrived in her new home. About the third day after I left, during my nightly call home, Charles casually said, "I saw Joan's bank balance of thirty-two cents in Miami, so I decided we had better open an account for her here. There will be times when we will not be home that she will need money to pay the man who mows the lawn, etc., so we opened one today." I said, "Fine, honey. I've always given her money to have her own checking account—ten dollars or maybe fifteen dollars. When her small needs use it up, then I replenish it." I casually asked, "How much did you give her to start the checking account?" Charles replied, "Two hundred dollars." I nearly fainted, and when I had recovered enough to get my voice back, I almost yelled, "Charles, . . . Honey, . . . you didn't really, did you? She'll blow it all before I get home." Charles reassured me that she was a very sensible girl and he wasn't concerned about her at all.

Charles met me at the airport when I returned from this trip during the early morning hours. I was still sleeping the next morning when Joan went to school, so I didn't see her until she returned home in the afternoon. After greeting me she casually said, "You'd better give me some money for my checking account, because the balance is low." My heart jumped into my mouth and I said, "What did you do with the money Dad gave you?" She looked at me with complete surprise that I should even ask and said "I blew it!"

I nearly died. Can you imagine the emotions I felt at that particular moment? Here I was a bride with a teen-age daughter and I wanted Charles to love her. And the first thing she had done was to really "blow" all the money he had given her for a checking account. I wanted them to get along, and I certainly didn't want to have problems right off the bat, yet here one was!

On a tour there is no way to predict the amount of cash to be received. Some love offerings are large, and some are very small, so it's virtually impossible even to imagine what the money will be that I bring home. I could have very easily taken enough money out of my purse and given it to her, and Charles would never have known, but was I being loyal to him if I did this? Not only that, I wouldn't have been honest either, and much as I love my daughter, I looked at her and said, "That's your problem. Tell Dad when he gets home."

Joan looked at me momentarily like I had stabbed her. Here was her beloved mother who was going to stick to her husband and wasn't going to worry about what her dad might say to her! But she saw something else . . . she saw loyalty to the man I married. She saw loyalty between two people that God had made one. She saw loyalty between Mother and Daddy in a way that she knew she would never be able to play one of us against the other when she wanted something. She saw Mother and Daddy united as one, and she loved it!

115

Don't you think for a moment that your children do not know when you're not loyal to each other, and don't think for a moment they respect you for it either. Children like to know that they can depend on their parents being united. They like the security of knowing that their parents are loyal to each other, and will defend each other at all costs.

Be One

by Frances

When God made us one, He gave us the right to the greatest happiness in the world, because there is no beauty or state of being on earth to compare with a marriage that God made and keeps because of its perfection. Charles and I enjoy doing *everything* together, and why shouldn't we when you realize that God in His original plan created man and woman from the same flesh, because He intended for our desires, our ambitions, our aims, our hopes, our likes and our loves to be the same.

Had God intended for us to have a difference in these areas, he would have created us in a different way. He could have taken a leaf, a flower, an apple, and from one of these created the creature called woman, but He did not.

For the express purpose of creating us to be *one,* God did a unique thing. The Bible says God "formed" Adam, but it says: "And the rib . . . made he a woman." It doesn't say He formed the woman *from* the rib, but it says the very part He removed from Adam's side, made He the woman. Had He formed the woman, there might have been something added, but the rib was made into the woman.

In other words, there was no outside substance, only an integral part of the man was used, therefore women are literally one flesh with man. When I realized the truth of this statement, I experienced a more tremendous closeness to Charles than I had ever realized before. No wonder a man should love his wife the same as he loves his own body, because she really is a physical part of his body.

There are many ways by which I could point out how oneness is partially achieved. *All* the things you do together are helpful toward the total oneness—attending functions together, spending recreation time together, working in the yard together, discussing finances together, and disciplining the children together. But I'm going to concentrate on two things which can bring more genuine oneness than anything else.

Charles and I enjoy doing everything together, but probably one of our greatest and most exciting times is the time when we are praying together. There was a time when I couldn't imagine that praying would be exciting (back when I was an unredeemed sinner). But probably the closest times we have are those when we are praying together for the things on our hearts.

Many couples pray at the side of their bed. We have prayed there upon occasion, but our most intimate, personal, fervent prayers are those when we are wrapped in each other's arms as we lie in bed together. This is the very last thing we do at night before we go to sleep because we want God so very close to us as the last thing of the day.

We thank God for the fabulous day He has given

us, and because all our days with Him are fabulous, we have lots to talk to Him about, and lots of things to thank Him for. After we finish rejoicing with Him, we begin to pray for the requests that come to our minds concerning the people with whom we have come in contact during the day—who either need to know the Lord, or who need a closer walk with Him.

Then as the Holy Spirit brings back into our minds the conversations and letters of the day, we pray for our children and for those who have shared their burdens with us over the telephone. We pray for those who have shared their heartbreak with us through letters and for those we have shared the plan of salvation with during the day. We pray for business and household needs. We pray for specific needs in the churches we have spoken in. We pray for individuals whom the Lord lays upon our hearts. We pray for our future engagements—for the churches we'll be going to. We pray for the book we are writing at that particular moment. We pray for the areas of our lives which need improving.

We don't have any particular order of prayer at bedtime, but we just pray as God's Holy Spirit leads us. Many times we thank God for bringing us a fresh, new message from His Word. Oh, there are just many, many things to thank Him for. We have also discovered that by audibly saying the words, "God, I love you," or "I love you, Jesus," we receive a fresh awareness of God, and it brings the presence of God so near and dear no one could ever doubt the fact that He is right in the room with us.

Practicing the presence of God is such a beautiful, precious experience as we do it at bedtime. It's marvelous all the time, but especially so at bedtime, when the lights are out, the house is quiet, and there's a stillness that seems to make it easier to really hear God. As we lie in each other's arms and pray, we ask God to wrap His arms of love around our arms of love, and to keep us safe through the night. The most wonderful way in the world to go to sleep is knowing that God's arms are wrapped around both of ours. There's a closeness to God that's supernatural, and there's an intimacy and closeness between a married couple that really can't be accomplished any other way. Probably the most glorious moments of our marriage have been as we prayed. Somehow prayer strips away the veneer of our lives and in our honesty to God we become even more honest with each other. As we draw closer and closer to God we draw closer and closer to each other as we become truly one.

If there is any hostility or misunderstanding between a couple, there's no better way to break it down than through prayer in each other's arms. God is so forgiving you can't help but be in the same forgiving mood when you're talking to God with your arms around your mate. In bed, there's nothing to disturb—no outside influences to take your attention away from prayer and consequently hostility or misunderstanding when lifted to God becomes in reality an apology to the other person and since it's filtered through God, the beauty of the moment is unsurpassed.

Oftentimes as we are praying at night, God's

Holy Spirit who has been praying for me, brings something into my mind which I may have forgotten to tell Charles, and as I talk to God about it, Charles also hears, too. There's something about night prayer that brings all the things of the day into recall. What more blessed way is there to relax than just talking to the One who cared enough to let His Son die for us? Just to know the power of God's love is the best sleeping pill I know of, and what a beautiful way to slip into sleep, with God.

Although I've concentrated in the beginning of this chapter with praying in bed, we pray constantly for everything as it comes up. As I mentioned in the chapter "Right Now" of my book *Hot Line to Heaven,* the time to pray for most requests is at the moment they arise. As situations come up in Charles's business, we pray *right then.* As things are brought to our attention when we're home together, we pray *right then.* And if during conversation with each other, God reveals an answer to a problem, we thank Him *right then.*

The other night at the supper table Charles bit his tongue, and even though we had to laugh a little as we were praying, we asked God to stop the bleeding and the pain, and *instantly* it left. We didn't wait to see what was going to happen, we just laid down our knives and forks, and prayed right on the spot. Both Charles and I are so dependent upon each other to pray if there's anything the matter with us at all. I should also include in this area our daughter Joan, whom I have failed to mention until right now concerning prayer. When we are all three at home, the prayer circle includes all three of us, and it certainly gives all of us a greater feeling of love for each other.

Lots of times I think the problems exist because people don't depend on God for *everything*. That's why they don't know the excitement and closeness prayer brings to a family relationship. We wake up in the morning talking to God, and we keep talking to and thanking Him all day long. The Bible says to pray constantly and the fact that Charles and I share every prayer burden with each other, means that our closeness to each other grows every day. When someone calls concerning a problem, if Charles is talking, he asks me to pick up an extension and to agree with him in prayer as he prays. If I am talking to an individual, Charles picks up the extension and we pray jointly for the person involved. Many times I will pray part of the prayer and Charles will pray the balance, because what God doesn't put into my mind, He seems to put in Charles', and our prayers are always more complete because the two of us pray together all the time.

And talking about prayer, did you ever realize if the two of you are concerned with praying for the needs of yourself and other people, there won't be time to criticize each other? Because we look to God for everything, we have found that things just don't come up that might be a source of irritation in our marriage.

Now, how do you get around to starting this kind of relationship? Maybe you have never prayed together—and when I say together I mean "out loud." Maybe you have a reserve about doing this. May I suggest you start right now, or whenever your partner is home next? Just hold hands and say, "Thank you, Lord, for making him my husband"— or vice versa, "Thank you, Lord, for making her my wife." You don't know what it will do to your relationship to God, and you can't imagine what it will do to your relationship with each other.

What if you have never prayed out loud? How do you start? Where is there an easy starting point? Well, first of all, if both parties are interested in making the marriage really exciting, you won't have a communication gap, so it won't be as hard on you as it is on those couples who have reached a real problem in this area. Talk to each other, and suggest that you start talking to God nightly. One of you will have to start it, and while it should be the husband, if he's not the prayer warrior in your house, the wife can start it.

Now here's an interesting thought to remember. If neither of you have made a practice of praying out loud, remember the male ego is stronger than the female ego and your husband might not want to admit his weakness in this area. So you may have to start the praying, and may I plead right now for you not to show off. There is nothing that will turn a man away from praying in bed faster than to hear his wife come out with these beautiful, carefully practiced words that would make anything he tried to say amateurish. Make it simple and very, very short, and then just say, "Honey, you've just got to help me." Ask him to give you some ideas as to what you should pray about.

Remember while this is going on that God is real

and is waiting and anxious to hear from you. Think on prayer in this manner: If you and your husband had some friends whom you hadn't seen for some time drop in and visit you, you would tell them the things that had happened since you last saw them, wouldn't you? Try talking to God just as you would with some other friend. Get yourself a good book on learning how to pray. There are many excellent little tracts and many, many wonderful books written on this subject which can help you tremendously.

The trouble with too many couples who don't pray together is they wait too long to begin praying. They wait until their marriage is close to hitting the rocks. Then as a last minute little flurry to hold things together, the wife will decide that prayer is the answer. Maybe the husband won't even listen to her very well by this time. Perhaps he will reject almost anything she tries to get him in a good mood. As a result one or the other or both will be annoyed with their mate to begin with. Even if you are annoyed to the limit with your mate at this particular time, I dare you to go up to him or her, hold hands and say, "God, will you let my partner know I love him even though we are mad at each other?" and still be mad when you finish praying. It just can't be done, because there's something about God that brings love into a relationship, and not anger.

If yours is one of those marriages which has waited longer than it should to start praying, just imagine God in heaven smiling on you right now and saying, "I'm so glad you're going to start talking to Me about your problems. I've been waiting for such a long time for this because I know the solution. And don't worry about what you say to Me. You don't have to be clever or trained because the only thing I want from you is your willingness to call on Me knowing that My love can solve the greatest problems. Now, My child, what did you want to tell Me?"

You see, that's the way God really feels. He wants His children to be happy. He wants us to talk to Him so that He can give us the answers to the things that bog us down. Because God is a giving God, He longs to give! He wants to give you the special warmth of His love. He wants to heal your broken heart, and give you peace. He wants to get rid of the communication gap, and all the other things that keep a marriage from being perfect.

It's futile when we try to run our house without God because then we run into trouble. Listen to what the Bible says, "Unless the Lord builds the house, they labor in vain who build it; Unless the Lord guards the city, the watchman keeps awake in vain. It is vain for you to rise up early, to retire late, to eat the bread of painful labors; for He gives to His beloved even in his sleep" (Psalm 127:1,2).

Unless the Lord builds your house you labor in vain and worry all night long. Think of the sleepless nights in homes which have been built without God. To His beloved God gives sleep.

There have been times when one of fell asleep while the other was praying in bed because we have been so blanketed with the peace of God it was impossible to stay awake. Try praying for oneness, will you?

And then there's the matter of reading the Bible. This is an area where the American family has grown very lax, probably because of the pressures of current day by day living. We love to read the Bible together. Our daughter Joan prefers to do most of her reading alone. Charles loves to have me read to him, and it happens that I love to read, so we always reserve a portion of the day for reading the Bible together.

One of the good things about this in a husband-wife relationship is that as God reveals things to us, we both are on the same spiritual plane or on the same spiritual wave length. It isn't a question of one of us understanding something, and the other one being completely in the dark about it. Not only that, as God reveals to both of us, we have a greater understanding of what God wants us to know in His personal letter to us that day.

Once in a while when we are on tour, we may not have an early speaking engagement, and so we stay in bed beyond the normal time, and just wallow in God's Word. It's amazing again what it does to our relationship as we discover *together* the things that God has for us.

I am often reminded of the verse "Long to grow up into the fulness of your salvation; cry for more, as a baby cries for milk" (1 Peter 2:2,3). Eat God's Word—read it, think about it—and grow strong in the Lord and be saved! You know, the more I read the Bible the more I am convinced that God gives us every single instruction we will ever need in life to live the exciting abundant life Christ promised us.

When a couple is not on the same spiritual level, some really great problems can arise! This is why in our spiritual life we should share everything together. Let me show you what I mean.

When Charles and I were first married, I had a whole year's tours scheduled which, of course, I had to keep. Because God gave us such short notice as to getting married, Charles didn't have time to prepare to go with me, so I had to go alone. I would go off on my tours, and get on a high spiritual plane. Even though I would call Charles nightly and write him daily, sharing the miracles that were going on, he didn't feel a part of them. And I would come back from a tour just bubbling over with things to tell, and Charles would feel, "so far behind me spiritually," as he put it, that it drew us apart momentarily until we got back into the routine of the nightly praying and Bible reading and sharing.

This happened in spite of the fact that each telephone call we have ever had has ended in prayer. We have probably spent more money on telephone prayers than anyone I know. But somehow or other, the fact that I was out there experiencing tremendous things for God wasn't helping Charles to maintain the same spiritual level. We really went through the fire in the beginning months of our marriage, but God taught us some invaluable lessons, and one of them was to keep on the same spiritual level. Charles goes along with me on most of my tours now and we share the bountiful blessings of God together and stay on the same wave length.

You probably will not have the same problems

that we have had because of our being unable to be together on my tours in the beginning, but on a different scale you can have the same problems—or the same solutions, depending on which way you want to look at it. Maybe there's a "Lay Institute for Evangelism" coming up in your church or in your town. Don't one of you go alone—BOTH of you go, whether you feel like it or not. There is nothing worse than when one partner goes to a spiritual blast and comes back breathing fire, and the stay-at-home partner is cold and unresponsive. It doesn't help either way.

Many times a wife feels restricted because of children. Take some good advice and get a baby-sitter and go with him. The same thing is true if a good evangelist is coming to town—*both* of you go together. If there's a special service at the church, *both* of you go together. When I see couples really having the beautiful marriage God intended for all of us to have, I always find out they are on the same spiritual level. If one of you is going to watch Billy Graham on TV, then the other one should watch also, so there will be a definite oneness between you.

Maybe one of you teaches Sunday school, and the other one has not been called to teach. Well, I would do one of two things. I'd either help out the one who teaches any way I could, or I'd just be right in there, backing the teaching one up with prayer. Or maybe your husband is on some committee in the church. Listen intently to the way he shares with you the problems and, if possible, see if you can't get on the same committee. In a lot of churches there are enough committees to keep couples apart several nights a month.

Anything that separates a couple is not good. Well, you say, one of you is an extrovert and the other an introvert. Great! Let the extrovert do the talking, and let the introvert do the praying, because if you let the extrovert go alone, pretty soon you won't even understand what he's excited about. Some of the greatest team teaching done in churches today is done by the man and wife teams where one is the extrovert and the other is the introvert.

And how do you read the Bible together when one doesn't even read the Bible? Get a good translation, and let the "reader" read out loud to the other. Both Charles and I have our own Bibles which we mark separately and independently of each other, but we've often recommended that the really interested one should start the reading. Pick a particularly exciting passage and read it to your mate. Read from one of the newer translations that are so easy to understand and be sure to read one of the really exciting promises that God gives. Here is one little verse I happened to see as I opened my Bible right now. If you've had a problem come up during the day and didn't know the exact answer, and you've asked God to solve the problem, you might try Ephesians 1:8: "And He has showered down upon us the richness of his grace—for how well he understands us and knows what is best for us at all times." How can anyone question God when He knows what is best for us at all times? And how can we be concerned or worried when we know that God holds our future. He certainly knows what is best for us at all times, so this leaves it up to us. Do we want to seek His way?

Another verse I just happened to see is in Galatians 4:7: "Now we are no longer slaves, but God's own sons. And since we are his sons, everything he has belongs to us, for that is the way God planned." Just think—God owns everything, and since we are His sons, everything He has belongs to us! What an absolutely powerful thought! Who could help but rejoice at a statement like that?

In our business life, if we have a problem, we go to the boss or someone who knows the solution. Think how simple it is in the matter of living to be able to go to the One who has the right answer to all of life, and He has put it down so beautifully in His Word.

I just happened to glance at a little note that Charles had scribbled and put in for me to consider and I think it's a real gem. "We never grow tired of loving each other because we never grow tired of loving God. The more we love Him, the more we want to be near Him, and the more we are together, the more we want to be together. I love you, Frances!"

Becoming divided instead of one is an insidious little game the old devil likes to play. It can start out so simply and easily. We have had many people who try to separate us for various reasons, but we always stick together like glue because we enjoy being one. People in churches many times try to take me to one side and Charles to another, and one of the greatest examples of this came when we were special guests at a military function. Since I was the speaker, I was to sit with the commanding officer, and Charles was to sit with his wife, and nobody at the head table was to sit with their marriage partners. When I was advised to sit next to the commanding officer, Charles politely but firmly held onto my arm and said, "No, sir, my wife and I are one, and we don't sit apart." The officer's wife explained, "But this is military protocol, you have to sit like this!" Charles replied, "I'm sorry, protocol or not, *no one* separates me from my wife."

It so happened they had given me the rank of a two star general during my stay at the military base, so I teasingly looked at the commanding officer and asked, "Pardon me, sir, but does a two star general outrank a full colonel?" The audience howled as he had to admit it did.

Then I asked, "May I pull my rank just for tonight then and sit with my husband?" Then I looked at the crowd and said, "I think it's immoral when they want a man to sit with someone other than his wife, and I think we ought to complain to Washington, don't you?"

And would you believe it, THEY GAVE US A STANDING OVATION BECAUSE WE STOOD FIRM ON WHAT WE BELIEVE, THAT GOD MADE US ONE!

by Charles

Ephesians 5:31 says, "That the husband and wife are one body is proved by the Scripture which says, 'A man must leave his father and mother when he marries, so that he can be perfectly joined to his wife, and the two shall be one.'"

All the love Frances and I have, started by it flowing through God and Christ Jesus. That was the only thing we had in common as we began to get acquainted, and we still talk constantly when we are together about nothing except Jesus. Our spiritual bodies were so solidly welded into one even before we physically knew each other that we really were one in Spirit. That same beautiful love quickly became one physically, and the welding of every fiber of our flesh became just one.

This oneness of spirit and flesh was brought forcefully to my attention as Frances spoke to exciting groups, experienced miracles and shared this excitement with others as I stayed home to do the more routine work of my business life. As she told me of the thrilling adventures and how much she wished I could be with her, my desire to share everything with her was so strong that I even let it grow unknowingly into a form of jealousy. What was really happening was that we were being pulled apart spiritually by good things, but nevertheless pulled apart. It was such a strong pull that my description to Frances was that it hurt as badly as though someone grabbed a piece of the flesh of my arm and jerked it away from the bone. Since God truly made us one, the hurt was the same as a physical pain in my own body.

One adjustment that has taken place in our marriage, which I'm sure isn't too different than in almost any marriage, was that Frances was relatively well known in the circles in which she traveled and spoke, while her books added extensively to her growing popularity. Then all at once she had a husband who was not so well known and when we were together she had a choice of two ways to go. Every human has a strong mechanism called ego which goes around hunting for recognition unless this vacuum is completely filled with Christ. Frances loves her assignments from God and she is very exciting. It is much easier just to drink in this excitement and love which others so freely give to her, but Frances chose another way. She began before we were married to draw us together. She could have chosen to operate alone as one, or she could have chosen the route she did, to have the two of us walk as *one*. Today we have an exciting joint ministry.

Our wedding announcements said we were "united one in Christ" and for this reason we believe complete oneness in each other and in Christ is the foundation necessary for the ideal marriage.

A tremendous oneness can be enjoyed by couples

who are united in planning a business together. The success, failure, bumps and thrills can be absorbed together to build a unique oneness of enjoyment in a business. Some men feel that *his* business is none of *her* business. But it really is amazing how observant and perceptive a wife can be if the work is done together as a joint venture. This working together can be adventuresome in seeing how well the couple can get along and love each other, but you need to work at love as well as love to work. To succeed in business requires sincere, devoted, hard work. A marriage will be a success if given as much effort. If men would put as much into making their marriage work successfully as they do in their business we would have less bankrupt marriages.

Men often put money above everything else, claiming they want "to give my family everything," but such money is too expensive. Its love can cost you your soul. Its love can cost you your wife and your family. Even if you claim you don't love it, but let habit or priorities cost you times with your wife and create a separation between you and your wife, it's not worth what it can buy for you.

Be Married

by Frances

No book could be written about an exciting marriage unless somewhere in the pages there was information about the sexual relationship, the culmination of marriage. "Sex is the sun of our marital universe and from it stems attitudes—good and bad," says my husband. Since neither of us are doctors or psychologists, we would like to just share with you what we have discovered.

From the female side, I had been widowed for many years, and had apparently put all of my sex drive into building a business. Then all of a sudden came a love for a man I didn't even know, a man I had never had a date with, but whom I married because God told me to. We probably had a lot more problems facing us than the average couple because of the unique way we were brought together (The full story is in *My Love Affair with Charles*.) and yet we had no real problems because we had our eyes on Jesus.

Please remember that I had never dated my husband, and had only seen him three times in three days, some eighty-eight days before we were married. Because our romance was so totally of God, we depended on Him for *all* the answers. Before our marriage, and even before Charles came to Miami for our wedding, I prayed and asked God to make me the kind of woman that Charles needed. I asked Him to let me respond to Charles in exactly the way he needed. Having been "man-shy" for so many years, I really had no idea what was to be expected after fifty, but all I knew was that I wanted to be the woman that Charles needed, and I asked God to make it so. I had built a wall around my heart many years previously, and I wanted to make sure that God took that wall away.

After our wedding and reception were over, it was about 3:30 in the morning and we were both exhausted from a hectic day of packing and getting ready for my return to Houston with Charles. As we drove away from the church, in my complete state of exhaustion I almost panicked. I decided I was hungry (the usual bride trick), but there wasn't any place open at that hour, so there wasn't any place we could go except to the hotel where Charles had made reservations. Once we got inside the room, I looked at Charles, and I think I realized for the first time that my husband was a male human being. I nearly bolted for the door, but I couldn't because he had his arms around me, holding me tightly. Anyway, he was between me and the door. The wall that had been around my heart for so many years grew to sky height in those brief moments. I was as rigid as a board. Charles asked me if I wanted to sit down and I said, "No!" and the wall got higher and higher and I guess I just silently screamed out, "Oh, God!"

Then, in the greatest display of tender love I have ever seen, Charles gently kissed me again and whispered in my ear, "And the man and his wife were both naked, and *were not ashamed*" (Genesis 2:25). The beauty of the moment was unreal, because God had spoken right through him, and the walls of Jericho came tumbling down!

Somehow or other, we are all taught modesty (and rightfully so) when we are young, and somehow or other it turns to false modesty and stays with us all of our lives unless we are brought to the truth by God's Word alone. Isn't it a shame we do not teach our children that with a husband and wife, there is nothing except beauty in the way God created us. This one little verse of Scripture did as much for our marriage as any other one I can think of, and God gave it to Charles at precisely the exact moment I needed it. It was only when sin had come into the lives of Adam and Eve that they were ashamed and considered nakedness something that needed to be covered. The Christian godly attitude about sex does not need to be covered.

One of the most tragic conditions that exists in a marriage occurs in regard to the sexual relationship. Many women, because they haven't been healthfully grounded in a knowledge of sex, use sex as a privilege they give to their husbands, instead of seeking what the Bible says about the fact that when a woman is married, she has no right over her body. It belongs to her husband and, by the same token, her husband's body belongs to her, and each of them should love each other's body as they love their own. It's very pathetic when we counsel with people to hear a woman say, "Well, he was mean to me, and so I just fixed him. I wouldn't go to bed with him." Then she goes on to say, "When he gives me my way, then I let him have what he wants."

Right now I am thinking in particular of a woman who had great problems in her marriage. She had a particular mania for things. In other words, she liked a lot of attractive things around her house. Her husband was a struggling young businessman, and was trying to be very careful in his outlay of money until the business really got on its feet. This annoyed her very much. Coupled with this was the fact that he very often worked late many nights in the office and this really bugged her when he didn't come home to have dinner with her. So then she would put on a little pouting act, and allow no sex whatsoever. When the time came that she really wanted something like a color television, a new car, a new rug for the living room, a new sofa, a new washing machine, or something like that, then she would very self-righteously allow him to do the thing that God intended as the most beautiful part of oneness between a man and his wife. With the majority of couples who have problems in this area, the woman uses the sex act as a bargaining item, or a bribe to get her way about something or other.

I would like to throw this little thought in right now. What are you really doing at this point? Is a woman accomplishing what she wants to with her husband? Oh, you may get the new car, or the new rug for the living room, or the new washing machine, but actually what you're doing is making a prostitute of yourself, because you are selling your body to your husband in return for something that you think you want. If there was anything in the world I wouldn't want to be doing, or be guilty of doing, it would be selling my body to my husband. You may disagree with me on that, you may think that has absolutely nothing to do with prostitution, but let me tell you this, the woman on the street sells her body for money. A wife who is guilty of bargaining sells her body for "things." There is absolutely no difference. It's just the price that is different—that's all!

Look at 1 Corinthians 7:2-5, "The man should give his wife all that is her right as a married woman, and the wife should do the same for her husband." It does not say that the man should give his wife all that is her right, and that the woman should *sell* to her husband what is *his* right. It goes on to say, "For a girl who marries no longer has full right to her own body, for her husband then has his rights to it, too; and in the same way the husband no longer has full right to his own body, for it belongs also to his wife." And now listen to what it says, "So do not *refuse* these rights to each other." The Bible says, and I repeat, "*do not refuse* these rights to each other." It says to *give* all that is yours to your husband.

You know, if women just believed that, and would quit this bartering business with their husbands (and that's exactly what it is) we would have a lot happier marriages.

The interesting thing is, you can't barter with God. You can't say, "Well, God, if you'll do this for me, I'll do that for you." When you serve God you have to *want* to give to God. Then the fantastic thing is, when you *want* to give to God, what He gives back to you is just completely unbelievable! There's no bartering with God. You have to want to serve Him first, and then serve Him without wanting to get anything back.

The same principle applies in marriage. If women would get over the idea of bartering with their husbands and selling this piece of property which they think THEY own, well, it's the same principle as it is with God. You can't barter with God, and you can't barter for a happy marriage. I have never seen a marriage that's happy when the woman sells her sex for a price, regardless of what it is. Maybe it's just making him wash the dishes at night. This doesn't make any difference, you're still just haggling about the price, and there's absolutely no difference at all between you and the woman at the well. Jesus so beautifully said to her, "Go, and sin no more!" Doesn't the same thing apply to any of us who have withheld rights from our husbands? Shouldn't Christ be saying to us right now, "Go and sin no more"? Give to your husband, in love, what rightfully belongs to him, and I guarantee that he will give back to you abundantly.

by Charles

The devil seems to start sex education very early in the lives of children and *true* sex education reaches the mind of a child too late. I can vividly recall the dirty stories, sinful impressions and implications that the big boys used to tell us little guys, and we were fully convinced and indoctrinated that anything that had to do with sex was sin. It was told in a way to tempt us. In spite of this atmosphere, somehow I managed to find a purity about sex and that it was a natural God-given human trait that was not intended to be talked about in shame.

We recently counseled with a teen-age girl whose parents were not Christian and apparently fought with each other constantly. Her concept of intercourse was that it was to occur only for the purpose of having a child and no more frequently than that and for no other purpose than that. She could only see a picture of dirty germs being injected into her body and she was determined that this would never happen to her, so she had planned never to let her husband touch her. All her babies were to be adopted!

What a sad mistake we parents can make by not openly talking to our children at the right age about a subject of which we need not have shame. Certainly they should be taught that it is a modest subject when discussed in mixed company. But why should we skip hastily past many pages of the Bible and say we had better not talk about that to our children? Why not skip the Lord's Prayer? Is it any wonder that children have an attitude that sex must be sinful and dirty because they have been taught to avoid talking about it the same way they have been taught not to tell dirty stories, or lie, or murder? Frances and I want to live long enough to claim every blessing and promise God has for us, and sex is one of the good things. God certainly didn't make a mistake in this area, although many times by our attitude we act like He did.

Frances told you in another part of this book about the joy and fulfillment we get from praying together in bed the last thing at night with our arms wrapped around each other. Why should sex be apart from prayer? Since God created man and woman for mates and designed and constructed us with the intimate desires He did, then for us to attain the highest, most beautiful relationship, we go to God in prayer. The smutty stories I heard while I was little seemed to be a prerequisite to sexual relationship. The Bible says, "Dirty stories, foul talk and coarse jokes—these are not for you. Instead, remind each other of God's goodness and be thankful" (Ephesians 5:3,4). Do exactly this, and God will bless you with the most beautiful relationship anyone could dream of. If you are physically sick and you pray for healing, why not try prayer for a healthy sex relationship and see what happens?

144

As a starter for sex education and a way to have an exciting marriage, just think of the title of each chapter in this book and see if they are not essential ingredients to an exciting sexual relationship: *Be* Loving, *Be* Considerate, *Be* Honest, *Be* Forgiving, *Be* Loyal, *Be* Patient, *Be* Courteous, *Be* Desirous, *Be* One! Put them all into a marriage with Christ as the living center and you will have the most beautiful sex life in the world as the most powerful demonstration of love completed in a human body.

I just read Frances' part of this chapter on selling your sex. I agree with her 100 percent in what she said about this being a form of prostitution. But I would like to add an additional male viewpoint right at this particular time. Someday you may discover to your dismay that the price you charged was so high that your husband has gone shopping elsewhere for a better bargain. In case you are not aware of this, this is a characteristic of men and one of the main reasons they do it is because their wives put too high a price on their sex.

I would also like to add another thought. God made man to be the aggressive one of the two in marriage, but even the most aggressive man likes to know that he is loved and wanted. How long has it been since *you*, the wife, were the one who started the lovemaking with your husband? Men like to know they are desired. Men, in spite of all their blustery qualities, like to know that they are loved and that they are attractive to the one they love. We like to know that you want us just like we want you.

How long has it been since you greeted your husband when he came home at night, with a kiss that said to him, "Let's go to bed, honey?" even if you are surrounded by your children and guests for dinner, including his boss. Just remember that he's not going to carry you to the bedroom right that minute. But the evening is going to be a delightful one because in the back of his mind all evening long he's going to carry that very special thought, "She LOVES me! And she thinks I'm desirable!"

I also want to say this to the wives. Many women have said they're afraid to kiss their husbands or to let their husbands kiss them because right away they get ideas. This isn't true at all. So many times women think this and use this as an excuse. If a situation like this exists in your family, why don't you look at yourself? Are you really withholding the things from your husband that he has every right to expect? If you expect him to be faithful and loyal and loving to you, then he has the right to expect the same thing back. No wonder he's reacting in a way that you might think is animal—if you're not giving him, and I mean *giving*, not selling to him, what rightfully belongs to him. If he feels constantly cheated, then the least little bit of kindness or affection on your part is going to make him think, "Aha, this is the night." And it really isn't that he's a beast at all. If you will keep him satisfied, then you will not have this problem. He'll never know whether another woman is pretty or attractive or glamorous, or anything else because he'll be so satisfied in his own little niche that he's not going to have ideas about anyone else.

So many times there is another little characteristic that goes along in this same vein. A wife may think, "I'm not going to go to bed with him tonight." So the evening is spent either arguing and bickering or making sarcastic, cutting remarks so that he will have no desire for love play. If you want to destroy the man who is your husband, this is a marvelous way to do it.

Many years ago a friend of mine told me that he really felt he was completely sexually impotent. He divorced his wife and married another woman and he said to me later, "You know, there's nothing wrong with me at all, except just the cutting remarks that my first wife made." This applies equally to men and women.

I think, too, that fear can cause a man to suddenly lose his preparedness to enter into this intimate relationship. The imbalance characteristic in a lot of men and women which results in the man being prepared (ready) before the glands of his wife respond, can also work the opposite. The man can lose quickly the climax of his readiness before the wife reaches hers. If this has happened once, a tenseness or fear can cause it to happen again and again. Their blame for failure to have a perfect, beautiful relationship can bounce in both directions.

We are born with a nature to blame the other party for our weakness or for a situation for which neither is to be blamed. A solution of this requires close communion and a deep desire to please the other. Again, trust in God to put within each spouse love, patience, courtesy, kindness and complete unselfishness as the key to peace, joy and happiness.

And God will give this if we ask Him and let Him control all phases (including sex) of our lives.

If you really want to have a beautiful sex relationship, you shouldn't just start one minute after you go to bed—your entire life should be lived in an atmosphere of love. To the men I would like to say that if you are loving and kind all the way throughout the evening and throughout the day to your wife, you're creating an atmosphere of love, which is so vital and necessary to the perfect sex act. If you have been criticizing her during the evening, you can't expect her to respond to you, can you? If we live in an atmosphere of love, then when it's time for the sex act, it will have been started and completed in an atmosphere of love, which is exactly the way that God intended it.

It may seem trite to write this next sentence because every marriage book has the same thing in it, but there is so much truth in this, I want to put it down anyway. If a man will learn to understand and respect the way his wife functions best as a partner in the marriage sex act, and will do the things that are necessary to put her in an attitude of love, he'll discover there are a lot less problems.

by Charles and Frances

We need to really appreciate the fact that God created this part of marriage for the ultimate in "oneness" between couples. God created it in beauty and love and it should be enjoyed in the way He created it.

The Bible says, "Give, and it shall be given unto you" (Luke 6:38). God didn't say, "Get, and then give."

God says, "Give, and it shall be given unto you." That's a beautiful thought. Let's take it into our marriage, shall we? Let's take it not only in other parts of our marriage, but let's take it in this most beautiful part of marriage.

Men, why don't you take your wife in your arms right now and just give her a real sweet kind of a kiss and say, "Honey, what are your needs? What can I do to make our relationship more satisfying?" And then, wives, in this same desire to please, seek to find what he considers ways to better satisfy *his* needs. Be completely honest with each other, but be loving in your desire to please. If we think only about serving the other one, and wanting the very best for our mate, living and loving will both be exciting.

Well, you've read our innermost thoughts about marriage. We were blessed because we both put Christ first in our lives before we were married. Understanding what God intended marriage to be gave us a head start on a lot of marriages. But what if your marriage is sagging right now, where do you start to get it where it should be?

If your marriage happens to be one in that category, we'd plead with you right now to read this final part of the book *together*. There are some questions you need to be honest about and answer right now as husband and wife.

1. Do you really want to make your marriage a success? You must want to make your marriage a success before it can be; just as you must *want* God before you can have Him.

   He_____ She_____

2. Do you really want to get the most out of your marriage, or will you be content to just "get along?" Charles says, "Do you want to eat steak, or are you content to eat garbage?"

   He_____ She_____

3. Are you willing, for a period of six months, to do your utmost to make your marriage what it can be? (With no reservations)

   He_____ She_____

4. Are you willing to forgive and *forget* all the things that have been stumbling blocks in your marriage up until now?

   He_____ She_____

5. Are you willing to keep in mind at all times, for

a period of six months, the idea of "What can I do to make my partner happy?"

He_____ She_____

6. Are you honestly willing to throw your prejudices down the drain for a period of six months concerning ideas that you have right now which are creating the problems you are having?

He_____ She_____

7. Do you honestly want to bridge the communication gap?

He_____ She_____

8. If an argument comes up, will you do your best to see that your spouse wins the argument?

He_____ She_____

9. Will you let God speak to your marriage by individually and then together reading the "Love" chapters (1 Corinthians 13 and Ephesians 5:20-33) at least once a month?

He_____ She_____

10. List the five things you could do for your mate to make him or her happier than he or she is right now:

He_____ She_____

1. _____ _____
2. _____ _____
3. _____ _____
4. _____ _____
5. _____ _____

Begin now by doing these five things.

If you can honestly (both of you) say "yes" to questions 1-9, we'll give you our suggestion. If you cannot honestly say yes, throw this book away and go on battling with each other. Be satisfied, then, with only a portion of what God wants you to have instead of a "double portion."

If, however, you both have said yes to all the questions, right now, start the same place where God starts with salvation. He forgave our sins. So each of you ask the other to forgive whatever has caused problems in your marriage, and then bury them in the sea of forgetfulness. Start your marriage over right now with a beautiful clean slate!

Be in Harmony
With God's Plan

by Charles and Frances

If we were to list any single *Be* attitude as more important than any other, there would be no choice except this last one of being in harmony with God's plan for your life. Living in harmony with God's plan makes husband and wife in harmony with each other. God's love and love between a husband and wife equal oneness.

We often look at the world of today with all of its multiple problems, and thank God we are Christians and know the answer to life. When a man and a woman are not in harmony with God's plan, they cannot possibly have harmony with themselves. Things just don't click right, and it seems as if the purpose and meaning in life get all mixed up. The things you have planned never seem to quite work out the way they should. This is because a lack of harmony with God creates a lack of harmony within ourselves. We were created in the image of God and when we failed to fill the spiritual need or vacuum in our life, we cannot possibly hope for the most out of life.

We both believe with our hearts and souls that all the problems of every marriage could be solved if both individuals would put their total faith and trust in God. Over and over again in our travels we see homes where one or the other is a dedicated Christian and the second one has been turned off religion and problems are numerous.

In the first place, until both individuals actually know about and accept God's love, they will never be able to love each other to the degree that is possible or intended when we love through God's love. We are not talking about a superficial acquaintance with God which we can get through occasional church going or giving. Rather, we refer to the full realization of God's love flowing through us as we learn to walk moment by moment with Him. We have faced many situations in our first year of marriage which could have been completely disastrous had we not been centered in Christ. Notice we didn't call them problems. Instead, we called them situations, because that's what all problems start off with. Then if the situations aren't resolved, they become problems. When the situations arise in our marriage, we take them immediately to God before they become problems.

We would like to quote a section of Scripture which we read often.

"And now just as you trusted Christ to save you, *trust him, too, for each day's problems;* live in vital union with Him. Let your roots grow down into Him and draw up nourishment from Him. See that you go on growing in the Lord, and become strong and vigorous in the truth. Let your lives overflow with joy and thanksgiving for all He has done. Don't let others spoil your faith and joy with their philosophies, their wrong and shallow answers built on men's thoughts and ideas, instead of on what Christ has said. For in Christ there is all of God in a human body; *so you have everything when you have Christ"* (Colossians 2:6-10).

Every time we read that particular passage of Scripture we get spiritual goose pimples all over, knowing that we have everything because we have Christ. How could marriage be anything but perfect, when you have everything! And when God specifically says that we can trust Him for each day's problems if we live in vital union with Him, how could we fail to do otherwise? It's such an easy solution to all problems, just to give them to God. But there's not much point in giving them to God until you understand that God wants YOU before He can take care of all of your problems.

When the love of God flows through the marriage partners, every sense is sharpened, and this makes marriage a far more exciting thing when all senses are tuned to the highest pitch. God has so much to offer every married couple, we wonder why we do not accept His love at an early age.

Last night we read in the paper where one out of every two marriages will end in divorce. What does that say? It says to us that if we want to see our marriage last we had better make sure that our hands are tucked in God's hand, otherwise we won't have a very good chance of success. But how could anyone ever want anything else? Until you know the beauty of God's love, you can *never* love your marriage partner to the fullest.

We have seen many marriages completely on the rocks with people absolutely incompatible. We saw them lifted to the highest plane because they turned to God. The capability of a human being to love with God's love so far surpasses human love there is nothing to compare it with. God's love gives security, trust, faithfulness, compassion, beauty, understanding, peace, joy, contentment, plus much more to those who will accept. Couples who spend time searching for growth in God will neither have time nor attitudes for arguments and criticism.

How does this relate to you? Where is the starting point? There's only one place to start and that is in your personal relationship to Jesus Christ. If BOTH of you are not in harmony with God's plan for your marriage, you can never achieve the ultimate, and since God made you one, your desires in this area should be mutual. If you honestly answered yes to the questions asked previously, throw down your barriers or stumbling blocks right now and remember you said you were willing to do your utmost to make your marriage what it should be.

One of the biggest stumbling blocks to every person reading this book right now with problems in their marriage, is a preconceived idea of what Christianity is. I'm going to ask you to throw out of your mind the ideas you have on church, religion, or whatever category you want to put them in, and think instead of God's love. I am sure you know the verse in John 3:16, "For God so loved the world, that he gave his only begotten Son. . . ." Before we go any further, I want you to listen to the very special way God said it to me, "For God so loved *Frances* that He gave His only begotten Son, that if *Frances* would believe in Him, she would not perish but have everlasting life." Now I'm going to ask each one of you to say *out loud* this particular verse, putting your name in the two places where I put mine and see what God says to you.

Did you hear the soft, sweet whisper of God saying that He loves *you* so much that He wants you to be in harmony with His plans so that you will be eligible for all the fringe benefits that He has to offer and which He gives us? Most men when they apply for a job are interested in the "fringe benefits" and the retirement plan. God offers both in a much greater way than any earthly employer—fringe benefits for daily living, and eternal life for your retirement plan.

Did you hear God say that He wants to come into your heart through His Son Jesus, and to live His life through you? Did you hear the beautiful voice of God saying, "Let Me do it My way?" Did you hear God saying, "Cast all your cares upon Me?" He does care for you. Did you hear God saying to you, "Let Me have your life and your marriage and I will give you rest"?—Rest from the personality conflicts you might have, rest from the financial problems you have, rest from the physical problems you have, rest from anger, jealousy, quarreling, harsh words, bad tempers, discouragement, frustrations, hatred, dishonesty, gossip, worrying and fear.

The beautiful thing about God is that He wants us to quit trying to fight our own battles and rest in Him. He wants us to put our hands in His hands and trust Him to take us through all the problems of life. He wants to do it for us! Think of the tremendous magnitude of that statement. *God wants to do it for us!* He wants us to put our lives into His strong arms, and rest in His love. He will meet all the problems we will ever have to face and then we'll be free. He says, "Ye shall know the truth, and the truth shall set you free."

Think about yourself right now as a prisoner locked up in a jail with no doors, and no possible way to escape. What would you want more than anything else? To be free, of course. That's what God wants to give you—freedom to be happy, freedom from fear, freedom from bad dispositions, freedom from all the things that cause you misery in life.

You might ask, "How is all this accomplished? How do I find God's love and plan for my life?"

God is offering it to you, and all you have to do is just accept it because the gift is free. Jesus has already paid the price for it. In Revelation 3:20 Jesus says, "Look! I have been standing at the door and I am constantly knocking. If anyone hears me calling him and opens the door, I will come in and fellowship with him."

RIGHT NOW just imagine that Jesus Himself is knocking at the door of your own heart, right where you are. He is asking you to let Him come in. Many times we have head knowledge of the Bible, but we don't have the "heart" knowledge, because we have never made a personal commitment to Jesus, and never asked Him to come into our lives. Isn't that a beautiful thought to know that Jesus Christ, the only perfect man who ever lived, wants to live His life in and through you, regardless of how imperfect you are. All you have to do is to reach out and say, "This is what I want."

Even as I write this last chapter, it is an awesome thought to know that Jesus lives His life right through me. And do you know why I know He lives His life through me? Because I asked Him to. In simple childlike faith I just asked Him to forgive my sins and then to come into my heart and live His life through me. No one could ever argue with me about the reality of Jesus because He lives in my heart.

You answered the questions and said that you would be willing to throw out all your old prejudices for a period of six months. Did you really mean it? And are you really willing to try the only way that will ever end your problems? Then I am going to ask you to say a simple prayer right now, asking Jesus to come into your heart. You can use your own words if you want, or you might pray the following prayer, remembering it is not the words that count, but it's the desires of your heart:

"Lord Jesus, resurrected Son of the Living God, I NEED YOU. I ask You to come into my heart and live Your perfect life through me. Forgive my sins. Take ALL of my life and make me what YOU want me to be. Take our marriage and make it what You want it to be. We put You first in our lives, our marriage and our home this very day. Give us love, more than we've ever had before to be able to meet whatever comes along in life. Thank you for supplying our needs. Amen."

Where is Christ right now? If you believed what

you prayed, you can honestly say, "In my heart." If you didn't, then pray that little prayer again until you KNOW beyond a shadow of a doubt that Christ is in your heart. He will do what He says He will.

With Christ in your heart, read this book again and ask Him to guide you into putting these principles into your marriage and ask Him to let you practice your new idea on your "old" mate (who should now be renewed).

We have just realized a fabulous truth. We know why it's so easy to love each other. Because Jesus lives His life through us, we are really loving Jesus when we love each other.

Let's do something unusual right now, shall we? Let's say our marriage vows again.

Why don't the two of you hold hands, and look right into each other's eyes, and make the following vows:

"I, Charles, take thee Frances, to be my lawfully wedded wife, to love in a greater way than I have ever loved before, until death us do part."

"I, Frances, take thee Charles, to be my lawfully wedded husband, to love in a greater way than I've ever loved before, until death us do part."

"We, Charles and Frances, accept your love, God, and your forgiveness, and promise to put You first in everything in our lives. Thank You for giving us a born again marriage.

"Therefore shall a man leave his father and his mother, and shall cleave unto his wife: and they shall be one flesh" (Genesis 2:24 and Matthew 19:5).